D1636701

WITHDRAWN

A DOORWAY IN TIME

OTHER BOOKS BY HERBERT O'DRISCOLL

A Certain Life

Crossroads

Portrait of a Woman

The Sacred Mirror

A Doorway in Time

Herbert O'Driscoll

1817

Harper & Row, Publishers, San Francisco

Cambridge, Hagerstown, New York, Philadelphia
London, Mexico City, São Paulo, Singapore, Sydney

A DOORWAY IN TIME. Copyright © 1985 by Herbert O'Driscoll. All rights reserved. Printed in the United States of America. No part of this book may be used or reproduced in any manner whatsoever without written permission except in the case of brief quotations embodied in critical articles and reviews. For information address Harper & Row, Publishers, Inc., 10 East 53rd Street, New York, NY 10022. Published simultaneously in Canada by Fitzhenry & Whiteside, Limited, Toronto.

FIRST EDITION

Library of Congress Cataloging in Publication Data

O'Driscoll, Herbert.
A DOORWAY IN TIME.

1. O'Driscoll, Herbert.   2. Anglican Church of Canada—Alberta—Clergy—Biography.   3. Anglican Communion—Alberta—Clergy—Biography.   I. Title.
BX5620.037A33 1985   283'.3 [B]   84-48228
ISBN 0-06-066340-5

85 86 87 88 89 10 9 8 7 6 5 4 3 2 1

*For the Church of Ireland,
from one of her grateful children*

Contents

Contents

Acknowledgments

My thanks for the invaluable discipline exercised by my editor, Avery Brooke of Vineyard Books; for the encouragement of John Shopp of Harper & Row; for the typing skills of Carole McCreery and Sue Johnsen; and for the forbearance of my wife Paula and my family in the face of many hours of my being mentally absent though present in the flesh.

Preface

I suspect that it is not without significance that the word *remembering* can be formed as re-membering. By its very nature, the act of remembering is to offer a thing of patches, to try to put together again a once seamless garment of events totally and immediately experienced but now tattered by time.

This is even more true of the recalling of childhood experience. The very vividness and clarity of things remembered from childhood frames them in shining images rather than creating a flow of sequential remembrance. Again, the writer who recalls childhood and the readers who find that such recollection opens a door to their own childhood experiences must agree to recognize that remembering childhood events is not to write of the way things were so much as to write of the way a child saw, heard, felt, and gave meaning to things.

The idea for this book came one day when I was discussing with someone the elements that make up what people have come to call early Celtic spirituality. After the conversation, it struck me that much of what I have heard and read in recent years about Celtic spirituality refers to it as in the remote past. The assumption seems to be that it—whatever it was—ceased to exist as a living reality somewhere between the Dark Ages and the early Middle Ages. It then occurred to me that far from thinking of Celtic spirituality in this way, I had always assumed that I was a child of it by reason of where I was born and grew up, the south coast of Ireland. From that realization came these pages, offering not a historical sketch but rather a living experience of a tradition that Western spirituality, to its great impoverishment, has long tended to forget and recently, to its own enrichment, has begun to seek again.

Christ Church
Calgary
Alberta, Canada

1. A Doorway in Time

Dr. Samuel Johnson once said that it would not be possible to stand on the battlefield of Marathon without hearing the clash of long-ago arms nor to stand on the island of Iona without in some way becoming aware of the long history of sanctity that has found home there.

In my own life I remember one early summer in Ireland in the year 1954. I had to very soon make a decision, whether the future for me was to be there on that island where I had grown up and that I had never left, or in Canada where I had been invited to go. I had come down south to see family and one day with a friend I was driving through places familiar to me.

The further west you go in Ireland, the more frequently you come upon small buildings formed out of flat stones whose walls slope up to a sharp ridge. Usually in front there is a small, low entrance. Very seldom is there a window aperture. The total effect is that of an upturned boat. In fact, the black upturned boats called currachs that have been part of life on the Atlantic coast of Ireland for centuries resemble these buildings when they lie on the beach drying in the wind and the sun.

Nobody is really sure when these rude buildings were fashioned. Many were already there in the early Celtic Christian centuries, from the fifth century on. Some are contemporary with the Iron Age. They are called clochans (pronounced "cluckawns"), from the Irish word for stones. Many became shelter for solitary Christian hermits, living and praying, probably also weeping and wrestling with the dark night of their souls. In later centuries the stones may well have sheltered the fleeing felon, the retreating soldier, the wandering poet or the family homeless after eviction.

To such a place I came in that summer of 1954, crawling in from the sunlight under the low doorway and sitting cross-legged on the earthen floor. I was aware of a stillness in that small space, aware that that utter simplicity once sufficed for some soul who possessed the whole world of early Celtic Christian faith—an ecstasy that I am sure exacted deep valleys of depression in exchange for the mountaintops of joy it offered. I was aware that all that experience and tradition was mine, by nationality, upbringing, and deep desire. I carried it in my genes (a word almost unknown in the 1950s). I was aware of the endless journeying so much a mark of that tradition. Patrick sailing under the lee of Cornwall, Columba gale lashed off the stormy beach of Iona, Brendan on God-only-knows what lonely stretch of land beyond the westering sun. Wanderers they all were, and beyond them the earlier wanderers who sought the same God by other names, were moved by the same ecstasies and felt the same doubt and darkness and ambivalence as they searched for light on their way.

Into that tiny cell on that afternoon there came a host of those who in their time longed for home. To me there came John of Patmos remembering Bethany, Paul in Athens remembering Tarsus, Amos in Bethel remembering Tekoa, Isaiah in Babylon remembering Jerusalem, Abraham in Canaan remembering Haran. Having found them all in rich and timeless tapestry on the bare stone walls, drawn there by imagination, disciplined by groping prayer, I became aware that in spite of their longing for home, all had continued their journeying. Bending to go out through the low doorway I stood in the sunlight. From there I went down the hillside and across the sea and into life, bearing both my gifts and vulnerabilities yet offering both for acceptance, secure in the knowledge that I walked in goodly company and over well-trod ground.

I realize now that as I left the sunlight and entered into the shadows of that rude and simple dwelling, I was entering a doorway in time. Although I was to have a vivid awareness of images of a past taught to me since childhood, it was a doorway leading not so much to the past as to a level of reality freed from time. There are many such doorways swinging open silently and unexpectedly in our experience.

Many years after that experience in Ireland, in 1970 I was invited to give some addresses in Ottawa, Ontario, where for some years I had been priest in a parish. The present priest had asked me to give the homily at the Eucharist on Palm Sunday morning. In replying that I would like to do that, I had made a small request. My wife Paula was with me and since we do not often get the opportunity to sit together for worship, I asked to sit in the pew with her and to go forward to give the homily when the time came. This was readily permitted, so duly on the morning of Palm Sunday we went up the steps of the church and were welcomed and handed a palm.

I arrived at the pew holding a prayer book, a church bulletin, and the palm. I was not quite sure whether to hold it, slip it in the prayer book, put it on the pew or in the book rack. It was a familiar part of the year's cycle in worship. I had come to take it for granted as a mere object, so easily can we become blinded by routine and familiarity to the hidden doorways of the sacred.

I became aware of a voice, very much embodied in a familiar layperson, reading a story. It told me of an entry into a long-ago city, of Jesus of Nazareth being welcomed by those who carried palms. Suddenly with a clarity that I had never known, I was aware that it was no longer a long-ago Jerusalem I was hearing about, nor was it contemporary Ottawa where I was standing, but both had become fused into a timeless reality. It was not a distant remembered "they" who shouted "Hosanna," but it was they and we in one timeless company. In a few days we and they would together shout the timeless obscenity "Crucify!"

I looked down at the palm grasped in my hand and I knew for the first time what it really was. Suddenly I realized what the bread between the teeth was, the red wine stinging the throat, the water on the forehead, and the golden candlelight on the eye. I knew that all these things were time machines, devices to sweep away the gulfs we call past, present, and future, to set us in a timelessness where Christ and Cross, lakeside and Upper Room could become for us places where we could enter and touch and become so much more than the prisoners of mere memory, however fervent.

Thus opened for me another doorway in time. In saying this, perhaps it is important to say too that while for me those particular keys were offered in terms of the explicitly religious, there are keys without number that are not at all religious in any traditional sense of that word. Above all, the many worlds of music come to mind, but the doorway can be swung open by something as deceptively simple and ordinary as a change in the quality of light about one, the nuance of something said in one's hearing, the angle of a turning face. The sacramental prodigality of God is so much richer than we can conceive.

The pages that follow are an effort to express some of the doorways that opened for me, especially in my early years, making it possible for me to become aware of a very ancient heritage and affording fleeting glimpses of a landscape that I could never name but whose fields and streets somehow intersected with the places in which I walked every day.

2. Geography of Childhood

To grow up in the south of Ireland in the 1930s was to inhabit a sacred universe. It was, I realize now, to live in the last lingering twilight of a medieval and, to some extent, feudal world. It was not an ideal universe nor even a particularly moral one, as indeed time and events have frequently shown. It was, however, a sacred world.

Behind or hidden in the visibilities and tangibilities of the everyday, another level of reality was always assumed. The seen was surrounded by the unseen, which, to some people and at some unexpected moments, afforded glimpses of either its beauty or its terror, its gifts or its threat. In that Ireland of the 1930s, the door between the worlds had not been closed as it would be in most of the Western world by the late 1950s, only to open again in the resurgence of interest in the mystical in the 1970s.

In that world there was always the web of family, both nuclear and extended, long before those neat, impersonal sociological labels became attached to life and relationships. The houses of uncles and aunts stood within walking distance in the small city of Cork, founded in Norse times on the marshes surrounding the River Lee, on the south coast. Those homes were the scene of mingled and transitory intimacies and antagonisms but always unquestionably family. There were Sunday visits to the large red-bricked institution known as "The Home for Incurables" where lay my paternal grandmother. As I recall that name it occurs to me now how unyielding was the language of an older society—honest, unpretending, to us today un-pitying. Outside the city on a green hillside stood "The Lunatic Asylum." Elsewhere in the city was a building gently curtained and beflowered at its entrance but having stone-cut above the door the words "The Rest for the Dying."

My grandmother awaited my father's visits, and I accompanied him. She had high cheekbones and flared eyebrows, and her long white hair cascaded over heaped high pillows. Her blue-veined skin rippled and shone parchment-smooth as she placed new golden pennies in each pocket of my first new suit, her hands touching my body like gently whispering ghosts on the edge of being corporeal. To this day, I have never traced that custom she called "Hanselling," which she spoke of vaguely as "a protection." I suspect it was a custom born out of ancient fears felt in the forests and high places whose last remnants still ringed the city after centuries of decimation.

Distant but intensely real was my mother's home, a place of other grandparents, of uncles, aunts, and ever-multiplying cousins, the farm flowing up the side of a wide valley where it seemed always summer. At some level of perception, I was aware of other seasons, but they existed only in conversations overheard. Once in a dream-like way, I could see the fields white with snow, the calves coming to the buckets of feed taken by my grandfather, their tiny horned heads banging the metal in their eagerness to eat. For the most part, seasons other than summer came and went in another time and universe where adults lived a sterner and separate life. For me, days ended when oil lamps brought evening or when at the end of the driveway no longer visible in the darkness, the trees lashed and hissed in the night wind. In the morning there was water to be brought from the depths of the moss-covered cavern where the well lay. There was hay to be brought from distant fields, drawn by the swelling haunches of great horses on whose foreheads flies stood dark and thick. Infinitely distant, seen only from the fields higher up the valley, a blue mountain called Mount Leinster lay at the frontier of a passionately loved universe.

There had never been an industrial revolution. No secular structure, even governments, had ever succeeded in wresting real power from the church. No huge cities cast their net of traffic or communications across an intervening and diminishing countryside. The rhythms of life, to the small degree that they were not those of nature, were the rhythms of the sacred traditions. The silences and celebrations of my whole world told the sacred story. The mark of ashes on every Ash Wednesday forehead; the empty silent streets of Good Friday; the call of the Angelus at evening; the sheaves of harvest in the parish church; the thousands standing to watch the Sacred Host pass by, canopied and escorted by priests and soldiers, nurses and police, Boy Scouts and pipe bands—all spoke beyond words of Corpus Christi, the Body of Christ.

Beyond and behind the Christian story were the echoes and shadows of one even older. Mine was a society of long and vivid memory where, as with some of us when we personally age, the remote past seemed more immediate and relevant than the present events. Only fifteen centuries had gone by since the Noble One (which is all that Patricius or Patrick really means) had kindled the new flame of Easter near the palace of the High King in Tara. Before that fire there had burned a much older one, blazing before ever a single great stone had been lifted high on

Salisbury Plain to announce the Sun God and to measure his passage.

That older world was very real to a child. Two or three farms away from my grandfather's farm, there stood a grove of trees on the top of a hill. By then it was surrounded by a golf course, yet none of us trudging over those fields would ever think of walking through the grove. Golfers did not search in there for lost balls. No one asked or said why. It was unnecessary. A common understanding existed about such a grove, a common memory knew it to be sacred. A common instinct kept it inviolate.

3. An Ancient Battlefield

I remember a particular day; it was Saturday afternoon. The Wolf Cubs had gathered at a suburban bus stop near the church. The weather had cleared so we could have our outing. We clambered and pushed our way up the narrow steps to the top of the double-decker, running toward the front seats, there to shout and argue and laugh until the last of the city had passed and the green fields stretched ahead.

I realize now that on that Saturday afternoon in 1936, the city was still the creature of the countryside. The rolling green ocean of fields allowed the existence of the city as an island set within its eternal flow. To come out of the city, as we were doing that day, was to return to a home recently left. In fact to live in the city, one of about 75,000 souls, was not really to leave the countryside at all. Every morning, a mile or two away, while the city still slept, Mr. Cleary milked his cows, put the milk in a large churn with a silver tap, harnessed his horse to the well-sprung buggy, trotted into the suburbs, and delivered his milk door to door, measuring it from a shimmering aluminum pint container into multicolored and variously shaped jugs held for him by housewives, among them my mother. Faithful to ancient custom he always added a little extra, what he called a "tilly," from the old Gaelic word *tuilleadh* which means to give more, reminding one of what the Authorized Version of the Bible refers to as "good measure, pressed down, running over."

At the end of the bus route we were assembled into a

ragged line by our cub master. It was hard to keep us in line because we were excited. We were about to carry out a favorite Saturday occupation. We were going to play in the old fort on the nearby hilltop. We didn't call it a fort because, though as children we did not know it, Latin, ancient as it was, had always had an uneasy truce on this island, encountering a tongue as old if not older. We called the circular earthworks that surrounded the hilltop "the Rath."

Half of us would defend the Rath and half would attack. So the defenders began their climb up the side of the hill. It was pointless for the attackers to go up because we would then only have to leave again to scatter and take up our lines of approach. Eventually we hoped to succeed in taking a flag that the defenders had planted in the middle of the now grassy center of the Rath.

That day I was picked to be an attacker. The cub master repeated last-minute instructions and we scattered among the fields and hedges. Each of us was now alone in the silent afternoon. I looked up the sloping hillside to where the small white clouds moved across the sky from the southwest, bringing with them the warm breezes from the Gulf Stream. At first the world was silent. I was aware of my own heartbeat, quickened by excitement. Gradually I began to hear the rhythmic sound of a nearby cow chewing the cud, the calm brown eyes gazing in detached curiosity at this small human visitor lying in the grass. Far away, the sound of a car or bus engine carried on the air.

I was no longer a Wolf Cub. It was no longer 1936. I was a Norseman and it was the tenth century. We had come up the river in our longboats, moored them, and headed inland for this brief foray. It had to be completed swiftly because we had to return to the safety of the longboats before nightfall. Thus the next hour was spent, carefully making the approach, lying still for long periods, now and then hearing the shouts as another attacker rushed the defenses and was caught. I used the bushes, the hedges, the trees—crouching, sliding, creeping, running. I signaled at last to another attacker to create a diversion. As he did, three of us went rushing toward one of the gaps that time had made in the earthworks. We bottled up our shouts until we were inside, rushing toward the flagpole that stuck at an angle out of the grass.

To touch it, we had to run the gauntlet of defenders. Once tackled by a defender, we were "dead." We knew that we ran and shouted where others long ago ran for life and delivered death. The grass where later we gathered for a snack was rich in blood long since drained into the earth. In the distance some of the little suburban houses had radios in them, from which was coming news of Europe, the first sounds of a guttural voice bringing another barbarism to Europe as Germany woke from its post–First World War paralysis. But I recall that now as a man. Then it was something a child was totally unaware of.

One realizes now that in that Ireland of the pre–Second World War years, the past was primary. In spite of the growing reality that was already hinting of the dark flood to come, it remained so. As those years of boyhood were passing for us, Spain was being butchered by the clashing of two ideological tides, both born in the twentieth century. Its skies were shrieking with a terrible new technology of death. But for us in Irish classrooms, Spain was forever embalmed in its sixteenth-century glory, magnificent in its power, the sails of its galleons about to round the headland, always the potential ally in Ireland's eternal struggle against England.

It was as if a whole people had willed itself into occupying the past as the place of ultimate reality. Through all one's growing years one saw the countryside through a time lens. This was true not merely personally but for most of one's contemporaries. Even when one came to university, one was not yet fully freed of the past to enter the present as reality. To come to Dublin from the provinces was to stand in the great vault of the post office and read the haunting lyrical idealism of the leaders of the 1916 rebellion. There, while English artillery demolished the city around them, they embodied one of the most literate and romantic of all twentieth-century revolutions.

To cycle over the Dublin Mountains was to look for the tortuous journey taken by the young fugitives, O'Neill and O'Donnell, as they made their escape from Dublin Castle in the frigid winter of 1591, making it possible for O'Donnell to become the last of the old Gaelic kings and the bitter enemy of Elizabeth in London.

To arrive at Clifden in West Connemara, to cycle out on the narrow rough road to the headland, the wind lifting the great inlet into white horses riding the dark waves, was to instinctively recall the desperate efforts of the scattered remains of the Armada to make any harbor on that formidable and foreign coast.

To drive southeast toward Dublin, the fields of Meath darkening in the evening, was to look toward the distant mounds that had once been Tara and the place of High Kings. To round the Old Head of Kinsale, the small inboard-engined fishing boat bucking and rearing in the tumble of conflicting coastal currents, was to sail among the remembered masts of the great Spanish fleet that waited there in September 1601 for its Gaelic allies to march south, both fated to suffer a defeat that spelled the end of Gaelic military power and the end of Spanish dreams of empire.

To see the woods on the high ridges of the hills, dark green against the sky, sharply delineated by the centuries of deforestation, was to think of the legendary warriors called the Fianna and the baying of their wolfhounds as they crashed through the forest in pursuit of deer long gone from now stone-walled domesticated pastures. To see those same low stone walls, their worn tumbled lines delineating narrow roads and tiny holdings, the grassy plots between them scabrous and pockmarked with scattered stones, was to recall the work projects of the terrible famine years of the 1840s, memorials to the desperate efforts of the more compassionate landlords to breathe life into an economy already dead.

Thus did the present fade into unreality before the vivid images and what for the most part was the tragedy of the past. By its determination to use the past to give motivation and political energy to the present and future of the fledgling state, a government was helping to create a generation for whom by a terrible irony the past would become the present and memory would become reality.

I mention this love affair with time in the Irish psyche because of the double gift it brings. To me personally, it brings a sense of stability in the possession of a long story, but there are some to whom this same ability to accord all layers of time equal reality gives something else. It seems to provide a kind of embalming fluid for hatred and ancient prejudice. It can kindle an endless twilight where no battle is ended, no issue is ever settled, no revenge satisfied; where church bells forever toll of a thousand wrongs and no bell rings in the new.

We ended our Wolf Cub Saturday. Grass stained, earth on our knees, sticky fingered from jam sandwiches, we came down the hilly fields to the country road. Joining the main road, we tramped to the bus stop. Where the roads joined, there was a shrine. Recalled now, rather than totally taken for granted as in childhood, the eyeless face of the plaster-cast figure looked back to the long-ago martyrdom of some minor saint. The military skirmish it memorialized took place some years before I was born. Soon the world would writhe in the agony of another world war. The maps of a continent would be redrawn. Psychologically and technologically, human life would be utterly changed. The old recurring dream of Europe would be reborn as the Common Market. The Church would change beyond all imagining at that time. Far above the same fields where we awaited the bus, an astronaut would step out into the Sea of Tranquillity. Yet this shrine would remain through all those years as a focus of memory, an echo chamber for the shouts of men long dead and the rattle of gunfire long silenced.

4. Journey to Joy

Among all the images of human life, that of "journey" seems richest, most profound. For me there are three particular journeys, the first taken frequently in childhood, the second recognized now as preparation for the third. I suspect that they are inescapable passages in the universal human journey. For me as for you they can be given beginning and ending in places in an exterior geography, but the names of those places from which we traveled and at which we arrived are only outward signs of an inner landscape traversed. For me, the three journeys lie across that inner country as the journey to joy, the journey in fear, the journey to maturity.

It was early July 1937. I was nine years of age, my brother was five. We had just been told that we were going to Castlecomer the day after tomorrow. We were going to stay on the farm for five weeks. Later my father would come for two weeks.

To say that we were excited falls totally short of adequate description. We were in ecstasy. In some way easily forgotten in adulthood, we were experiencing a transcendence of time and place, of time because the concept of five weeks of happiness was for a child no longer merely time but eternity, of place because Castlecomer being, as my father had often said, a hundred miles away, was for a child placed in quite a separate geography.

Each moment of preparation was etched indelibly. All the previous day my mother washed and ironed, hoping for the sun to pour into the small backyard to dry the lines of garments set out in morning oblation. With tongs she took from the fire the red-hot stones that heated the iron. The piles of sweet-smelling warm clothes grew high on the kitchen table. In the evening my father came home from work. His role year after year was to pack the bags. He would achieve the impossible, not without various struggles and mutterings and exasperated comments, and finally it would be time for us to have a special midweek bath and go to bed early, where we would exchange ecstatic whispered conversation until sleep came.

In the morning we would savor the rare experience of taking a taxi. It would come up the hill street from the station, a large ancient American car, its own journey to Ireland probably the whim of some emigrant who had prospered and sent home a wondrous symbol of his success. To sink back in its huge interior was itself an adventure.

Thus we came to the bus station and all was piled on the sidewalk as my father went along the line of buses to find the bus for Clonmel. Eventually we were aboard, the driver and the conductor walking among us, enviable in their peaked caps, the conductor equipped with a large metal ticket dispenser hanging on a shoulder strap. The engine started, the bus shuddered into life. Waving to my father, faces pressed against the vibrating window, we were off.

Through the streets we went, over the many bridges that crisscrossed the great hidden marsh on which that ancient Norse city was once built; along by the railway station, then by the river for a few miles, passing Blackrock Castle and turning north through villages and towns that sing in the remembering—Tivoli, Dunkettle, Glanmire, Watergrasshill. More and more quickly the hedges flew by as the bus picked up speed between the villages.

Horses and carts, donkeys and smaller carts pulled aside into the long green grass at the roadside to let us pass. From time to time we slowed down, not quite stopping at a country store and pub. The door of the bus noisily swung open, the conductor seized a roll of newspapers and threw them with unerring aim toward the shop doorway, and we were off again.

Climbing all the time, we went through Fermoy, passed the army shooting range at Kilworth, our eyes widening at the odd piece of ancient artillery seen behind the line of trees. Somewhere on a hilltop a stone cross stood starkly against the sky, half hidden in mist. To a child, it was somehow "the" Cross, yet also I knew it to be a symbol of more recent agony hinted at in the replies of my mother. She, of course, was remembering the flying columns and the ambushes and the deaths all over north Cork less than twenty years previously.

Through Mitchelstown we went before turning east, the tires singing their high-pitched song, the voice of the conductor calling out the names of little towns, themselves a song in the joyous mind of a child—Ballyporeen, Clogheen, Ardfinnan. The blue distant world of the Knockmealdown Mountains rose away to the south, the rolling fields of Tipperary to the north. Turning under the dark bulk of Caher Castle, the fifteenth-century fortress of the Butlers, rulers of a great part of this southern province, we finally drove along the banks of the River Suir to Clonmel where lunch awaited followed by the thrill of another bus.

All through the long sunny afternoon we climbed the low range of hills that brought us out of Tipperary and into Kilkenny. Somewhere on the road down out of the hills there was a house with mysterious dark blue panes in its windows and a fish pond in the garden, both strangely exotic and intriguing. Year by year this house assumed

significance on this journey. Its unseen inhabitants began
to be clothed with fascinating possibilities. I imagined
myself inside the house, having skirted the fish pond and
entered the front door. I was inside the parlor amid dark
formal furniture. The sun, weakened by the blue panes,
threw strange patterns of light and dark on the floor.
Footsteps were approaching the door of the parlor. Suddenly before the stranger came, I was again back in the
bus and the house was disappearing behind the hedgerows.

By now it was early evening. My brother, somewhere
between waking and sleeping, leaned against me as the
bus rattled along the road beside the River Nore. The
Cathedral of Saint Canice sent its spire and its magnificent
Round Tower into the evening sky to welcome us. We
moved through the outskirts of Kilkenny city, swinging at
last into the square under the shadow of the great Anglo-
Norman castle of William the Marshall, the seat of the
Dukes of Ormonde. There across the square was the smaller
country bus to carry us the last twelve miles to Castlecomer.

There amid parcels from their days shopping in "the
city," my mother met familiar faces who said the familiar
things of friendship about how her boys had grown. We,
half blinded by the sun now low across the fields, gazed
from the front seat of the bus past the burly shoulders of
the driver, looking for well-known scenes, until we turned
the last corner and came up the straight stretch of road
that in turn became Kilkenny Street, its row of shops now
closed for the day. There at the corner stood the light
carriage we called a trap, the black mare between its
shafts, my uncle standing at her head. There were greetings, laughter, a flurry of cases and parcels, a climbing up
into the seats of the well-sprung trap, and we headed up
the hill out of the town.

Adult conversation was impossible, with our endless

questions. We asked about the farm, about the animals, about the stream through the fields, on and on until the high graceful wheels of the trap stopped in front of the house. Quick greetings were given to grandparents before the mad dash to the stable. The other horse stood in his stall, turning his head as we gingerly but affectionately stroked his haunches, his eyes shining in the darkness. From there to the cow barn, the hay barn, the pig's house, the apple orchard; on to the high wooden gate my uncle had made since last year. We swung it wide, standing on the flagstone ouside it that bridged the small stream where we would sail ocean liners made of six-inch slivers of wood. There, sloping up from us, an endless green land stretched away until it entered the long dark wood that crowned the slope and stood both as guardian and boundary of our world. Behind us and below us was the small town of Castlecomer, half hidden in the thick green trees that clothed the valley floor.

5. A Love Discerned

At the upper end of the square in Castlecomer a low wall topped by high railings defined the creamery. The yard was empty, the machinery was quiet, the morning voices silent. Dust swirled in a slight afternoon breeze where the feet of donkeys and horses had clattered a few hours before. Their dung was already hardening under the sun in the open area in front of the building.

I feared and was fascinated by the creamery. It and its counterparts in many small towns were cooperatives formed by a newly created republican government intent on bringing some efficiency and thus improving production in Irish farming. There the farmers brought their fresh milk, receiving in return skimmed milk for their animals, as well as the use of a cooperative price system for other farm supplies and implements.

Bringing the milk to the creamery consumed the precious early morning working hours so it was work for old men or boys. Sometimes it could be contracted out to a neighbor who needed the money.

That daily journey to the creamery was my time with my grandfather. We fulfilled the criteria for the task, he by age, I by childhood. To me, far from being a task, it was pure joy.

To begin the adventure, one must again climb the stairs to bed the night before. One must begin there because the anticipation of the morning journey began even before sleep came. There is another reason however. I wish in memory to again accompany my grandfather from night-time to waking.

The great black range had its sea coal packed down for the night, its fire glowing through the black bars. The *stirabout*—meal feed for the hens—was on for the morning. That night neighbors had come visiting—it was called "rambling"—after the evening chores. They sat smoking and chatting near the fire. The door to my grandmother's room was closed. The oil lamp smoked slightly on the yellow wall. I was reading *The Egyptian Wanderers*; I had found it in the small bookcase at the top of the stairs. It had been given to a granduncle as a school prize in the late 1800s. His name was written on the flyleaf in faded copperplate. The book was subtitled *A Tale of the Fourth Century Persecutions*. Forty years in the future I would stand on the southern outskirts of Beersheba, flanked by a dingy gas station and a cheap gift shop, looking south-west into the Negev, waiting for the four camels to emerge from the remembered inner landscape of childhood.

I was given a candle and told to go to bed. The treads of the tiny staircase were creaking and steep. At the turn on to the low and narrow landing, all light from downstairs disappeared and the shadows leapt and played as I lifted my candle higher. The door at the end on my left led me to the double bed that I shared with my grandfather. Later he would come with his candle, undressing quietly and donning his long heavy nightshirt. I felt the pressure on the bed as he knelt for his nightly prayers, kneeling where I had knelt an hour before. For us both, the action had a total naturalness in this little world as yet unbroken by dying gods or human invention. I did not realize that the memory of this quiet piety would come to me as a dream of grace among the secular fantasies of the faraway 1960s, when clever books would sell a new enlightenment announcing prayer as neurosis, sacrament as superstition, and God as only a memory. In that future desert of the spirit, I would remember the white close-cropped head of my grandfather, seeing it bowed in rapt unquestioning petition on the rough blanket. I would remember his rising and turning, the sound of his breath extinguishing the candle flame, the reassuring sense of his presence banishing the fear of night and releasing me to untroubled sleep.

Night's true banishment came with the sunlight pouring in through the small single-paned window high up on the wall, the crowing of the red-combed strutting cock and the sound of buckets banging in the dairy below this end wall of the house. There would not be, even in heaven, a single day brighter or fuller with unsullied joy than the first day of annual school holidays after one had arrived at the farm.

The churns were up on the cart, the sun glinting off their scrubbed aluminum. They were warm to the touch from the milk newly taken from the cows. Sacking covered the bench where my grandfather and I would sit. We were given the grocery order for the day, reminded to pick up the mail and the daily paper—reminders as unnecessary as rubrics in an ancient liturgy.

Crossing the farmyard, the iron-bound wheels crunched and squealed. We reached the gate, I turned to wave, the donkey broke into a canter, his harness jingling. The impetus would take us over a hump in the road, and we were on our way. The two miles to the town were mostly downhill. Sometimes we joined a neighbor, seldom passing, always saluting, perhaps remarking on the surrounding fields, particularly if the crop was damaged by rain or wind. We passed the new government cottages, slate roofed and stark, clotheslines stretching from them. Around them stood goats, rope hobbled to prevent them from wandering, their pointed beards moving as they chewed ceaselessly, their eyes dark and wise, their udders heavy with the tart milk that then only the poor drank but that would one day be the stuff of affluence and sophistication in faraway urban worlds as yet unbuilt.

We knew the names in every cottage, slated or thatched. Wherever there was a face looking out a window or over a half door, there was a salutation. My presence in the cart was itself a symbol of the returning season. "Abie's grandson is up from Cork," the voices would say as we passed. The season came when I was old enough to be allowed to take the reins of the donkey, feeling his dogged energy passing along my straining arms as I swelled with pride at this public responsibility.

Down the last hill we went, past the Captain's high wall. On the other side of the road the police station was half hidden behind its wall, a reminder of a violence distant from me by being before my birth but vivid and recent to all adults around me.

Hidden in cobwebbed thatched lofts lay guns glistening with the oil of romantic memories of youth and danger. If I had looked with older eyes, I would have seen the walls of the police station pockmarked by bullets under the new plaster. Men going to the creamery saluted one another but remembered other mornings when violence was sanctioned by a revolutionary government to which the Church gave grudging and qualified absolution, hearing in countless confessions the bloody secrets of side-road ambush and private revenge.

We were into the town then, bumping over the seldom

used rails of the train crossing, swinging left to take our place in the line of carts heading slowly into the creamery. My grandfather got down from the cart, moved around to chat with this or that neighbor. Rejoicing in the freedom, I presided, reins in hand, over the slow inevitable progress of the donkey who moved forward willingly, if only because he was nibbling at the straw sticking out the back of the cart in front of us.

Gradually we approached the heart of the operation. On a high stone platform the supervisor stood at an accounting desk. Behind him through the open doors could be seen the machinery that received the fresh milk and in turn dispensed skim milk. The high interior was full of steam and thundering with the noise and clatter of machinery. To a child, it was a fearful but totally fascinating place.

The supervisor's coal-black hair was streaked by the swirling steam, his Wellington boots glistened. I now realize that he appeared to a child as a kind of demon, standing with unassailable authority over a domain of fire and steel where churns were wrenched open as they crashed onto the stone platform, their contents hurled into the vast tank, the quality of the milk measured by magic vials that a white-coated figure dipped deep into the white, frothing flood. Then the arm of the skimmed milk dispenser would swing out, the churns would be positioned under its wet cloth sock, and the whole cart would shudder as the white steaming column of milk fell into their wide hungry mouths, filling until the bubbles foamed above the rims. My grandfather and I would replace the covers and move on, my heart pounding with excitement, my thoughts anticipating the next duties of the morning.

The post office was a symbol of a mingled history, the

red British crowns on the old boxes painted over with a patriotic green. That day it was full. The bare boards echoed with the tramp of farm boots. The government notices, printed in English and Gaelic, were yellow in glass cases on the walls. Only we children could read both languages and even we read haltingly in Gaelic as a new republic formed us to be the first Gaelic-speaking generation since the late seventeenth century.

We moved from the post office to a tree in the square where we tied the donkey. Then we walked to the news-agent where we bought an *Irish Times*. It was the paper Protestants tended to buy. "West Britons" some called us. The choice of a newspaper in that countryside labeled one with the same precision as a computerized report would later on in the century. To buy the *Irish Press* meant that you were passionately Republican, possibly Sinn Fein. It hinted that you were "out in the troubles" and indeed would go "out" again if there were more "troubles," the term "troubles" being a euphemism for the much uglier term "civil war." To buy the *Irish Independent* meant that you had mellowed, moved more to the political center, sought responsible government, probably were upwardly mobile in the modest sense possible in that limited econ-omy. To buy the *Irish Times*, however, was more than a statement about class. It was also a statement of religious identity. In that little town the *Irish Times* copies, few though they were, certainly went to the Captain's House, the rectory, the teacher, the bank manager, and the doctor, as well as to the Protestant farms, among them ours. In its pages would be the English cricket scores, the statements of Church of Ireland bishops, letters to the editor no less articulate but more passionate than those in the Times of London, not to mention the birth, marriage, or death of anyone whose birth or marriage or death we might be concerned to know.

Among the newspapers there stood on the newsagent's counter a jar of golden pillars, twisted foot-long pieces of barley sugar. Within that morning ritual my grandfather would ask me if I wanted one. Becoming increasingly deaf, he would usually not use words but would point and wink conspiratorially. We both knew that I was to consume the last half inch before we rounded the corner to the farmyard gate to face parents concerned about such city things as dentists and teeth cleanliness.

Sometimes there were other things to be gotten—a piece of meat in the butcher's shop, a few items in a grocery store also a pub—but eventually we turned for home again, heading across the railway tracks, up the hill, along the green tree-canopied road. Our progress slowed and the haunches of the donkey knotted and swelled as he began to pull the cart up the side of the valley. Sometimes we would get out and walk. Sometimes my grandfather would let the reins hang limply in his hands, the sun rising higher in the sky and warming his heavy country waistcoat. His head nodded. Gently, holding the half-consumed bar of golden candy in my left hand, I would take the reins from his sleeping fingers. I sat straight and very proud, assuming full responsiblity for him, for the milk churns, for the donkey and cart. I swelled with pride when a passerby cast a real or imagined glance and smiled. Now and then I snatched at the long waving grasses at the side of the narrow road. Sometimes in moments of riotous imagination, I pretended my depleted candy was a cigarette. I cradled it between two fingers and deposited imaginary ash to the wind with a brave flourish.

Thus within time, yet in a way that was a time out of

time, we rounded the last bend in the road before the farmyard gate. The donkey broke into a happy jog, the harness about him jingled, my grandfather woke, and we went crunching over the graveled yard to where my grandmother waited for him in her chair behind the white lace curtains, reaching in anticipation for her reading glasses, opening them with the white and twisted fingers of her pain.

She was forty when there came first a stiffness, then pain, then the necessity for a walking stick. Visits to the doctor brought only two walking sticks and, when necessary, the arms of sons and daughters. One day she left the kitchen and sat in the adjoining room. She was never to walk again in the next thirty years of increasing pain. During that time she and my grandfather continued their quiet love affair, rich with three daughters, two sons, and the memory of a child, my namesake, who would because of early death forever remain five years old.

Every day there were two particular periods during which they would enjoy one another's company. Sometimes in the late morning they would read the paper and comment about the world to each other. Later, when the work in the fields was over, he would again sit with her.

When she died, her body was buried in the churchyard, as was the custom of those days. It was also the custom of those days that such things happened without a child's involvement. My grandmother's death was a distant and mysterious event, seen with puzzlement only through the tears in my mother's eyes.

The following year, summer having come again to the farm, I came there on holiday. There came a day when we were to visit relatives considered distant in that small island world. As we drove through the town and over the bridge, I was in the backseat with my grandfather, my uncle, and aunt in front. As we drove past the gates of the graveled driveway leading up to the churchyard where the summer grass was high and green gold in the sun, my grandfather, thinking he was unobserved, pressed his face against the window of the car and with a small hidden motion of his hand waved.

Somehow I knew what he was doing. Our eyes did not meet. Nothing was said. I doubt that he realized I had noticed. But I have always been aware that for a boy, it was a moment of gentle but immense growing. Like a traveler who comes suddenly to the edge of a great escarpment and sees a country vast and mysterious and lovely, I came to my first understanding of the majesty and the vulnerability of human love.

6. Journey in Fear

High summer of that same year of 1937 and the men were in the fields. That particular day they were at the far end of the farm, across what was called the "Old Road" and then two more fields over. They would need their tea in the field so that they could stay there and use the valuable hours of sunshine to get the corn cut and bound and stacked.

In the oven was a huge deep apple pie, its juices running over under the crust. With it there would be thick meat sandwiches and strong dark tea. I was to be the bearer of these good things, but I was afraid. To reach my uncles and my grandfather, I had to venture beyond one instinctive boundary set about this countryside of childhood. I had to cross Cody's fields. They began immediately beyond the field beside the house. There were three of them between our farm and the Old Road and in each of them there was fear.

Like many childhood fears, these things are now recognized for the potent symbols that they were. Then they lay in wait, understood only as physical threat. Now that I meet them again, I recall that there lay in the third field that which was more than physical.

Sometimes when playing in the Barn field, we would go over to the high ditch that separated the properties. There was a stile, its three flat stones protruding from the earthen ditch as stepping-stones to the top. We could climb this and look into the unknown. From where we stood, a winding footpath, nothing more than grass flattened into the summer-day earth, wound across to a gap in the other side of the field. That gap, closed roughly by some tumbled barbed wire, opened on to another field, and so on into the distance. I had been over those fields on a few occasions but with adult company, never on my own.

With the large basket of food in one hand I climbed the stepping-stones, stood irresolute on top of the ditch, and climbed down the other side. While standing there, I had seen him. He was where I had hoped he would be, at the far end of the field, grazing quietly in the shade of a tree. The bull was large, to a child massive. I was aware of him as ruler of that territory where I was a trespasser. I did not use the footpath through the field. I skirted along the opposite hedge, stumbling now and then on the rough earth, fearfully keeping an eye on the object of my fear. Once he moved, turning his great head in my direction, making me freeze. The mugs rattled for a moment in the basket and the sound traveled in the silent insect-humming fields.

I reached the gap on the other side, found a way through the barbed wire, and headed out over the second field. Somewhere there I knew there was the stallion, restlessly moving around the field, his loud whinnying sometimes sounding across the fields at dusk. He was fearful to me in a different way than the bull. Somehow the bull was blind brutal force. The stallion was also to be feared for his power, but it was grandiose arrogant authority. Both were kings with unquestioned power to wield authority in their domain, the bull a barbarian monarch, the stallion a trumpeting romantic medieval king. Again the heat of summer was my ally. The stallion too was seeking the shade. As I passed, I could hear the shudder of his body as he shook the persistent flies from his skin, flicking again and again with his thick black tail.

Beyond the second field I began to approach a grove of trees. As the path entered the trees, the ground sloped very slightly, the sheltered grass was mingled with moss, the heat of the sun lessened, the ground was carpeted with mingled light and shadow. There to my right, half hidden by bushes and small trees, stood the ruined house. The roof, once thatched, was completely gone. The small openings for window and door showed thistles, weeds, and wild flowers filling the half-hidden interior. In the simple phrase "once living" written now spontaneously after forty-six years, I realize why a child felt fear. There is always something fearful about a ruined dwelling. Life has become death. Voices have sunk to silence. Movement has been stilled.

The road—the Old Road—was only a hundred yards away. It seemed much farther. Looking out at it from that glade was like looking from a darkened stage set into a brightly lit theater. I had learned enough Irish history to guess when death came to this silent place. It came halfway through the previous century in the guise of a demanding bailiff whose claims became more and more demanding and whose threats became more ominous. It came without disguise in the shape of constabulary, some mounted, coming to exercise the landlord's prerogative. There had been the harsh orders, the pathetic possessions naked under the sky, the torch thrown on the thatch, the cries of children, the impotent rage of men and women.

All this I sensed in the deceptive summer afternoon, silent yet full of the weeping of another time. The sound of that weeping loud within my imagination, sent me hurrying from the skeleton of the old cottage. Hanging heavy at my side, the basket slowed me, increasing the sense of threatening presence. There was a point at which high bushes obscured the nearby road. In their shadow there came for a moment the fear that by some dark magic the road would not reappear. Beyond the last trees there was a high five-barred gate, beside it a stile. I scrambled over it gasping for breath partly from fear, conscious of escaping from a separate world where things seen had become the devices by which the unseen had pursued me. I stood in the dusty road looking over to the sunlit field where I could see my grandfather and uncles at work. I had returned, a fearful traveler from a landscape they did not know.

Three years went by and I had done that journey a number of times. Its fears had lessened but I was never entirely at ease. The stile beyond the ruined cottage was always climbed with the slight sense of evading a pursuit all the more feared because it had no shape. But in mid August of the year 1940, my climbing over it became prelude to a journey that began in pain and ended in fear.

I had once again brought the basket to that same field. Nearby there was a cottage from which we got a large kettle of boiling water to make the strong brown tea. For the first time I was deemed strong enough to bring the kettle across the intervening fields.

In the cottage the kettle hung over the open fire, black from constant use, heavy, its contents scalding hot. I was halfway across the second field, just about to ford a tiny stream that bisected the field, when I stumbled, the kettle was jerked from my hand, the lid fell off, and the boiling water splashed down my barefooted leg. There were screams of pain, helpless sobbing. My uncles came running. I was put into the donkey cart and carried home. Someone cycled to the town and the doctor came. He had barely left when a telegram came. Telegrams were synonymous with bad news. My father was ill. We had to go home immediately. There is a memory of dread, hasty packing, the morning drive to the station some miles away on the main Dublin line, the journey punctuated by my own pain, the shared, unspoken family fear. When we reached the house, my father was too ill to welcome us. We climbed the narrow stairs to find him in bed and in considerable pain. Fear could no longer be left behind at the stile near the ruined cottage. It no longer was a thing of the fields, banished by sunlight and the sounds of reaping. This journey home was prelude for another. That journey would take place ten years later.

7. End of Innocence

The arch of the stone bridge across the river was high enough to hide the town square of Castlecomer until one had come to the center of the bridge. From there the small river flowed south between thick overhanging trees. In the still, dark water grew huge lily pads. Quiet ripples among them hinted of unseen creatures. Sometimes a bird cried out, its call echoing in the cavern of the trees.

Beyond the bridge, desirable by their age and location, there stood in comparative aloofness those houses that possessed more than a private prominence. Those were the houses of those public figures around whom the life of the community revolved. Shaded and gravel plastered, their Georgian doors and windows gleaming with black paint, there stood the house of the doctor, the house of the schoolteacher, the rectory, the house of the bank manager.

This was a world into which even the outriders of pluralism would not come for at least another quarter of a century. Each of those houses presented to the world an almost Olympian impassiveness. In my memory no child played before their curtained windows. If the gleaming brasses of the doorways ever swung open, I had never witnessed it. Each house had the high distinction of owning a motorcar. In front of the houses the great trees, planted long ago about the town square, ensured a further degree of shade, dignity, privacy.

Years later I would realize the hidden realities behind those lace curtains and blue hydrangea bushes. An old friend of my grandparents, aging and ill, desperately trying to survive with the aid of alcohol, that most treacherous companion of adversity; a merchant using the same device to ensure a constant camaraderie among his more significant customers while trying to live with a spouse's increasing depression, a condition not yet recognized as such in a society where Freud and Jung alike were lumped together among the demons of Modernism in the lexicon of a watchful church; a schoolteacher on the fringe of that little inner ring of town society, valiantly keeping up appearances on a very small salary; a rector gradually coming to terms with the realization that ministry would continue in that quiet place until retirement came, all the while remaining faithful and loving to his people.

Even now I feel the incongruity that that gracious and quiet town square was to be the place where I would encounter death, where my childhood would take one of those great leaps of experience whose significance is belied by their being of momentary duration.

Further from the bridge than the quiet houses the shops began. The first of those was the recently opened butcher's shop of Maurice Doyle. We must meet him because he was an Irish archetype.

Some years before this Maurice had gone to America. By then he had returned and, as all such returned emigrants, was regarded by the town as having about him that air of faint mystery made possible by a general ignorance of what he had or had not done in America. Maurice was a very typical affable roughneck whose romantic image was augmented by a broken nose, a wide gap-toothed grin, an incipiently nasal accent mingled with his native brogue, not to mention his own discreetly dropped allusions to cattle ranching in the western states. All this in a small Irish town where cowboy films had recently begun to be shown twice a week in the town hall made Maurice a somewhat exotic figure.

Small boys were captured by such romance. I was outside the shop, having walked down to the town for the everlastingly extra grocery item forgotten by my aunt in her morning foray to town in the pony and trap. It was a hot July afternoon. The square was almost empty because most men and women were hard at work in the fields. Maurice emerged and began to chat. I was from the distant city of Cork so by the magic of his charm we became brothers in urban superiority and worldliness, each aware of that town as a tiny world. I was intrigued by the slightest hint of distant adventure spiced by imagined villainy. We spoke of America, that faraway land whose very name had implications of freedom and riches and glamour for the generations of at least two centuries before either of us. We spoke of Texas, that place of high boyhood romance. Our conversation was replete with minor swears and blasphemies not allowed to a boy at home. We spoke of cattle drives and guns. There was, accompanied by a prodigious wink from Maurice, the merest hint of women, a subject about which my age gave me an emerging curiosity nourished by a vast ignorance.

I don't know at what moment Maurice made the decision to invite this Protestant city boy to witness what was about to take place in the shed behind the shop. Perhaps the showman in him longed for at least one spectator to help him give even slight reality to what today would be called a "macho" image.

We went in, over the sawdust-covered floor of the shop. We passed the great beef and pork sides hanging on their gleaming hooks, assorted entrails still attached to the rib cages. Crossing the yard, we came to a half door that Maurice leaned on and gestured to me to look in. Inside stood a large heavy bullock. The beast's head was lowered, the eyes regarded us balefully from above a large iron ring that held its nose and was attached to the floor by a chain. Around the chain the floor dipped in a hollow, at the center of which was a drain. I still did not realize what was about to happen.

Bidding me wait, Maurice returned to the shop. In a few moments he returned, grinning broadly and carrying a heavy double-barrelled shotgun. In his other hand were two shells. Only then did I realize that suddenly, without warning, I was for the first time in my life about to witness violent death. My heart pounded with a spasm of fear and excitement. There had been no previous such encounter. I had seen life already dead—a cat, a bird, a mouse. I had never experienced that terrible moment when life and death meet. Now it was upon me. Flight and fascination battled in me. The newly acquired device of closing my eyes to frightening scenes in the movies was suddenly of no avail. All this thundered through me as Maurice rested the great gleaming gun on the half door, squinted down its barrels, turned to me once with wild laughing eyes, and then hunched down for the kill. The bullock's legs were apart, its wide hairy forehead directly drawing my gaze. My eyes were riveted on this living creature to whom this sunny afternoon was to bring so sudden a death. The horrified waiting was shattered by the thunder of the gun. As if drawn together by his dreadful moment into a common death, Maurice's body staggered back from the kick of the gun. I was conscious of uncontrollable trembling while before us the beast shuddered, a great hole appearing in the center of its forehead. For a moment it continued to stand, then it toppled with a crash to the floor, its body threshing in spasm. In the stillness of the small town's afternoon, we could hear the trickle of blood as it stained the rusty grating and fell into the darkness.

This then was where the words of Genesis emerged into reality from the decorous Sunday morning worship in Saint Mary's beyond the trees. This then was what it meant to be given "dominion over every living thing that moves on the earth." This presumably was Peter on his Joppa rooftop bidden by a dream-encountered God to "arise, kill, eat." This then was Elijah on Mount Horeb, whom I had learned by heart in school, butchering the bullock to test Yahweh and applying the same knife to the butchery of the howling prophets of Baal. This was Abraham plunging the knife deep into the pulsating throat of the hastily captured ram, grateful that it was not the blood of Isaac his son drenching the rough wooden pyre. This by terrible metaphor was Jesus on the Cross, blood in the gleaming cup on the altar. This was the Sacred Heart pumping the lifeblood of the world above the little red lamp on the walls of ten thousand cottages and cheap row houses where the faithful dwelled.

My eyes turned from the blood-stained grating. Maurice's excitement had subsided. Saying that he now had work to do, he dismissed me, not with unfriendliness but with an air of being preoccupied, almost distracted.

I came out into the sunlight of the square and started up the hill out of the town, my small parcel in hand. My most shattering discovery was the nearness of the killing ground. Until today it had been infinitely distant. That animals were killed I had fully realized. Frequently there had been the frantic deaths of farmyard hens. My uncle would enter the hen house. In the unseen darkness there would be sudden sounds, the scrambling of claws, the beating of wings. He would emerge bearing the chosen bird, keeping the knife hidden from me as he passed.

Today had been a greater and more thunderous reality. Images of death seemed to be on every side where before there had only been things of the day taken for granted. Maurice himself assumed a greater significance for me. In imagination I looked through his eyes down a long gleaming barrel to see a human face rather than that of a beast. The small hospital that I could see from a certain bend in the road became a dreaded place even in the summer sunlight. I thought of the side chapel in the Church of the Immaculate Conception where I had sometimes seen a gleaming coffin attended by flowers and candles, awaiting its time for requiem mass and the slow walk to the graveside.

All the way home I was aware that things would never be the same again. I recalled the terrible high squealing of pigs that had so often punctuated sunlit days, carried on the breeze across meadows to a playing child. I realized I had been sheltered in innocence by a benign adult conspiracy, itself only too well acquainted with the faces and sounds of death. From now on, no such shelter was available. I had been taken beyond the first frontier of a mysterious country that lies around all childhood lands. From now on in my experience, sunlight and shadow would always mingle. I had encountered death. We had met in such a place and in such a way that my childhood became partner to what is perhaps death's most dreadful secret. As with the mystery of birth, death walks in the most normal and ordinary of places. The sacred child came to birth in the rude manger, the sacred bull came to the slaughter in the country shed.

8. Teller of Tales

During the years of childhood there was a hired man on the farm named John Brennan. With the eye of a small boy, I recall him vividly. He wore a scarf tied around his neck, a cloth cap, trousers precariously held up with binder twine, and boots with great holes in them. He smoked a clay pipe. He had a heavy mustache that dripped hot brown tea as his face emerged from a great steaming mug during a break in the summer haymaking.

I like even now to linger with John Brennan. I loved him. I use the word as seriously as a child always uses it. There was one whole day (and you know how long a summer day is in childhood) throughout which I became John Brennan. I announced this fact upon arising, refusing all day to answer to my own name.

He would often tell me of his far travels. To this day, I do not know for certain if he had ever been farther than Dublin, if indeed that far—all of seventy miles. But together we went in my imagination, and for all I know in his, to Afghanistan and Baluchistan. For some reason, these are the golden roads I particularly remember.

In terms of today's precise contracting between people, stated working hours, machines to clock in by, union rules to be observed, the contract between my family and John would be incomprehensible, certainly undefinable. The extraordinary thing was that it was so clearly indissoluble. That in turn did not mean that John was under any coercion to stay, nor was my family under any legal obligation to retain him. The bond was deeper, older, more subtle.

Without ever expressing itself in terms of feudal relationship and mutual responsibility, it acted on those ancient precedents. For instance, John was not a model of dependability. Sometimes in the morning he had to be sent for, and in the summertime I would be the one chosen to rouse him. I went with a mingling of fear and excitement.

Stories, if they are to be true to life, cannot always be linear and sequential, but rather convoluted, many faceted and prodigal with images that draw one from logical sequence. Such was the half mile of winding country road between the farm and John's cottage; thus while we set out on it, we will not arrive without detour.

Outside the double gate of the farmyard I swung right under the overhanging branches of the trees. The sound of my footsteps changed from that of the graveled yard to the baked clay of the road surface. Ahead was the first turn in the road, rising slightly as it passed the gate outside the Byrne's thatched cottage. There lived Jim and Mary and Maggie, a brother and two sisters, their total world that holding, a half acre defined from the greater surrounding meadow by a low hedge.

To a child, those three were already mythic, living in at least two levels of my awareness since they were the living figures in which I thought of the biblical family of Lazarus, Mary, and Martha in the house in Bethany. I would look with mingled affection and fearful curiosity at Jim, noting his pale skin and rather sunken albeit laughing eyes, wondering if by some strange juxtaposition in time he too had returned from some shadowed place whose steps were somewhere hidden in those surrounding green fields. That such thoughts presumed the presence of another in those green fields, powerful enough to stand in some sacred grove and to call Jim from the darkness, was only another aspect of the immense ability of childhood to encompass all that is received and to bond it into a single reality that gives time and space a perfect unity.

The cottage was thatched, not with the machine precision of its tourist counterpart today, but in the way of an ancient art even then beginning to falter. One entered by the five-barred gate at the roadside, moved through hens lazily picking in the yard, and came to the half door, hoping to be invited into the warm darkness within. Far above, the underthatch held its sea of cobwebs. Red coals glowed day and night in the huge recessed open fireplace that also served as stove and oven. Eggs warm from the hens lay newly gathered on the colored oilcloth of the table.

There beside that turn in the road that trio lived all their lives in utter simplicity. They went to the town for mass. Mary went more frequently for the few groceries they needed or could afford. In their long lives, not one of the three ever traveled as far as the city of Kilkenny, all of twelve miles away. Years later when as an adult I stood at the roadside, the cottage was gone. The yard and tended garden, even the gate leading into the cottage, had all disappeared, had again become part of the large meadow known as Back-of-Martin's. There was not the slightest trace that they had even existed. The change was so complete that I walked to the upper gate of the meadow, climbed over and went back across the field until I came to where I knew their half acre had been. Sure enough, the grass was a different quality where the cottage had stood. I knew then that their simplicity and warmth had touched my life in reality and not in a dream.

But all that is to travel forward in time. I was then on this stretch of road where the adult would not come for decades. I was bidden by my uncle to fetch John. I turned again to the assignment. The road was sided by grassy banks that rose to high hedges and hid the surrounding meadows. Now and again there was a gate that allowed me flashes of distant countryside. A sharp turn and I was at the long straight lane leading to John's cottage. Over it the trees met, creating on sunny mornings a leafy pavilion floored with mottled stone and earth. Under the skies of an afternoon thunderstorm, it became for a child an endless shadowed gallery leading to unimaginable terrors.

At the end of the lane, I came to an open area silent except for the quiet sound of running water and whatever breeze moved through this secluded green world. Immediately to my right the ground fell away into a deep gully. I paused there because I wished to postpone the waking of John. I knew from experience that there would be rage at the ending of sleep and I feared the unseen voice changed by its being called from the land between waking and sleep. I sometimes imagined that were I to look inside, I would see not John but some great shambling, misshapen thing moving toward the door, assuming magically in the daylight his familiar face.

I moved down the bank of the gully, postponing my task. There was a narrow path through the undergrowth. At the bottom I stood in a hallway whose magic would come again and again to my adult dreams. To my right was the small waterfall by which the stream dropped into the gully, falling gently down the sloping fields from the dark wood at the top of the valley. Above the edge of the falling water, the sun flashed through the white-backed leaves of a birch tree, assuring me that should I wish to return from this green half-buried world, I could do so.

The pool at the base of the waterfall was formed by the

surrounding banks and by large stones. From it the stream issued, leaping and chuckling over the gully floor. There, shimmering under the clear water, gleaming in the shadows, was a white form. It was the solitary white shirt that John owned. He wore it only for Sunday Mass and for High Days of Obligation like Ash Wednesday. From time to time, he carefully placed it in that running stream for washing. I had never watched him place it there, so for me the large white form under the water assumed a life of its own. It was fully stretched out, the sleeves spread wide and ending under stones, as did the neck. No Arthurian lake held more wondrous and mysterious possibilities than that tiny cleft among the meadows whose waters imprisoned that recumbent figure forever about to rise and send me shrieking along the whispering lane to the sunlit road.

One other focus of enchantment lay here. I came to it every day, white bucket in hand. It nestled below the descending bank of the gully and was reached by the narrow earthen path from which I could also look down on the stream nearby. The well had in recent years been given a shell of concrete that went down into the earth about five or six feet. Half of this circular shell came up out of the ground and with a concrete roof gave shelter to the well.

Already in that soft damp climate the earth was beginning to take possession of the concrete. Grass hung over it protectively as if to hide it, the moss was gathering inexorably, green and soft under the circular roof and along the concrete rim. The water was deep and still and clear. I would look long into the depths to discern the bottom, imagining a labyrinth of vast caves in which dwelled a lost race who could emerge through this drowned gateway between the worlds. I would place the white bucket in the water, shattering the image of my own face and returning to the immediate task of carrying the water home.

But before I could go, John had to be woken. I returned up the bank and was once again in the dark grove near his cottage. In fact, it was less a cottage than a ruin. All over the Ireland of those days were the ruined walls of primitive cottages, their thatched roofs long gone. John had partially roofed this ruin and lived in the solitary space where the chimney stood. Only once had I glimpsed the interior over the open half door. On that occasion I saw that he had marked off an area with some stones. Inside the area he had put some straw-filled sacks as mattress. A small crude table stood under the tiny window. On the wall hung a small framed Sacred Heart of Jesus. I never again saw the interior. It remained mysterious and fearful, the grove around it becoming in a child's mind both the home of a beloved friend and the lair of a fearful giant.

I approached the cottage, leaving the bucket by the rusty gate, rounding the end of the ruined wall that was open to the sky. I could see from there that the upper half of the door was closed. Grateful for that, I walked silently as I could until I knocked on the door, posed for flight if it should suddenly open. There was no sound. Taking a small stone, I banged again. This time there was an answering growl, rising to an angry questioning shout. I cried out, "John, Grandpa says you're to come!" Immediately I ran around the crumbling wall, out to the gateway. Taking the bucket of water, I walked as quickly as I could along the dappled lane beyond which the sunlight and the roadway beckoned. Reaching the roadway, I paused for breath turning home toward the farm.

Two things I learned from John that I never forgot. About a mile from the farm there was a crossroads. John told me that it and all crossroads were mysterious places. He said that one always had to make a choice at the crossroads and that every choice in some way changed the pattern of one's life. That is why there was an old legend that both God and the devil were very often at the crossroads, waiting. Each tried to ensure that the choice was made that eventually, by many other roads and after many other choices, would bring the traveler to heaven or to hell. One had therefore, he told me, to be very careful at crossroads. They were good places to make the sign of the cross on oneself, as one decided on a direction.

One evening of summer, when the haymaking was over and we sat together on the long granite stone outside the stable door, John pointed out to me that the earliest stars were beginning to appear. He then told me that, when the Angel Gabriel came to announce to the Virgin Mary her great vocation of giving birth to the Son of God, he waited for her refusal or acceptance. John told me that between the Angel's annunciation and Mary's acceptance, all the stars in the sky stood still, so important was that moment in time.

Years later, when I was in my late teens, my uncle had to sell the farm. I was not there on the day of the auction, but I was told of it. John was by then in his eighties. He had worked on that farm since he was a young man, my grandfather and he having grown old together in what, I now realize, was the last of a centuries-old feudal relationship of mutual trust and obligation. He had always lived in the small thatched cottage about half a mile from the farm.

The morning of the auction began a beautiful spring

day, the day when a farm that had been worked by four generations would pass out of the family. When the auction started, someone remarked on John's absence. In the last few years he had been able to do only very light work and only on a part-time basis. So my cousin went to look for him, walking the half mile of winding narrow road with its long grassy bands and high hedges.

John was lying in the long grass as if asleep. In the way that Paul in the Authorized Version of the Bible described the death of certain disciples, John had "fallen asleep." He had left the cottage to come to the auction and something deep within him, and a loving father above and around him, had decided that that spring day was the day for weariness to end and a great journey to begin.

9. A Gentle Patronage

When you left the town square in Castlecomer and crossed the bridge over the river, you were setting out on what could become either the main road to Dublin or the road to the town of Carlow in the next county of the same name. The distance to Carlow was all of fourteen miles—English miles, as anyone on a mid-August afternoon in 1937 would have assured you, the traditional Irish mile being longer.

About a mile beyond the bridge there was a curve in the slightly climbing road. From there we can look for a moment at that peaceful and traditional world. There was very little traffic. What did come was as likely to be a pony and trap as a motorcar. If the latter, it would be moving slowly enough for both driver and onlooker to recognize each other and at the very least to greet each other, perhaps even to stop and chat.

That same summer a friend of the family had bought a car. He had prospered and that purchase was the ultimate symbol of that prosperity. Within a few days of securing the new car, he invited my grandfather and my parents for a drive. My grandfather suggested a trip to relatives who lived in Bagenalstown in County Carlow. My grandfather sat in front, my parents and I behind. The total journey was traveled in low gear and never at more than twenty-five miles an hour. As we progressed, my grandfather and his friend discussed the passing scene. As my grandfather was quite deaf, this conversation was carried on very loudly. Who owned that grazing land over there?

What condition did it look to be in? What should those cattle fetch at the fair? How the farmer and his family were. How long it was since they had all met. Who had died. Who had married. On and on we went through a drowsy summer forenoon, until very slowly the land began to fall away, and with Mount Leinster across the valley from us, high and blue and serene, we slowly climbed the slope to the farm on the hilltop where shy and smiling cousins appeared to welcome us.

Such was the nature of travel on those country roads. By that particular spot the bus to Dublin would soon go by, vivid in red and white, smelling of petrol, its gears grinding, its tires on hot days singing sadly away into the distance. Immediately to our right, half hidden in the high leafy ditch beside the road, was a small rusty railing; behind it a concrete cross, its base festooned with glass-covered artificial flowers. They were whitened and soiled with the winters of a decade and a half. Once Thompson machine guns had rattled their harsh song of civil war there and men had died in the ambush of a convoy. The cross remained there mildewed by rain and time, unattended but for aging memorializers who would kneel on a chosen Saint's Day to finger their rosaries. Increasingly overgrown, it stood as a symbol of the violence and passion that lurked just beneath the outward peace of that and many other lovely valleys.

As with all rhythms of life there the passion and violence was slow to come to birth. Suddenly it invaded a generation, shaking and tearing at the fabric of its life, until the spasm was exhausted. Armies dispersed. Prisoners were freed once again. Pieces of paper were signed. Politicians sighed with relief. The demons were laid to rest. Then fading away into the green fields and small towns went all who were involved, doing again the simple things of everyday life, their women bearing the children who would learn the sad and bitter songs that would again waken the sleeping demons of violence and hatred.

In my teens my father and mother would sometimes speak of "the troubles." The euphemism I now understand to be an admission of remembered pain wishing to be forgotten. They would tell me of this or that person, very familiar to me, who had been "out" at that time. "Out" meant that they had been in the I.R.A. and had borne arms. For a child it seemed strange that this could be. I remember particularly a neighbor, a stout little man who daily rode a bicycle past our farm. He spoke in a high hearty voice and read the *Irish Press*. He puffed a little after the ride up from the town. I would look at him and try to see him as the Commandant of a Flying Column, which apparently he had been. I would try to imagine him putting his eye to the sights of a rifle, his short fat finger curling at the trigger. He would leave us, calling back a laughing remark to my uncle until he disappeared on his bicycle into the sun and shadows of the winding road. For a child he embodied the hidden violence that lay beneath my peaceful world.

The road to Carlow sloped through the trees toward the turn as we began to walk. On the right was the church spire above the high stone wall. The gates were open, the driveway way graveled between the lines of tall yew trees around the church. Half hidden in the long grass of early summer were graves I had been shown from earliest childhood. An uncle whose Christian name I bear and who died when five years old lay here. Our common name gave him the power to haunt me. It was not a fearful haunting. He came as a shadowy companion in odd moments of playful encounter. I did not know whether he shared my reality or I his wraithlike presence. The spot in the farmyard, the trench at the end of the hen house where he fell and contracted the sickness from which he died, was a place of particular significance for me. It was not so much a fearful place as a kind of door between the worlds where one might go through and play.

There were many such doors, avenues into the timeless that touches time, into the distance that is near. Such doors are especially accessible to a child but if we are watchful, they are given to us our whole life long. That churchyard and church was a place of some inarticulated joy for me. Sometimes I came there for evening prayer, walking the two miles from town with my parents. I recall an evening I was asked by the rector to pump the organ. I sat by the side of the organ's wooden pipes, pumping wind into the ancient bellows so that music for singing the songs of Simeon and Mary would not fade, leaving us standing in the almost empty church, the sounds of the gaslights hissing in the twilight. Perhaps the evening wheezing of the ancient organ was the breath of God calling me as an unwitting Samuel in the Temple to faraway priesthood, the rector my Eli, my mother a Hanna singing an evening hymn in the third pew.

Not far from where we sat and stood and knelt, beyond the heaving grass and slanting gravestones in the churchyard, there was another gate. Freshly painted, always open, it looked down a long, curved, graveled driveway. At the end, mysterious because it had been seen by very few, was the demesne, the Big House. It was no older than the eighteenth century, but in terms of what it was to the town, it could be drawbridged and battlemented. It was the home of a landowning family who came there from

England a couple of generations ago. Their loyalties were essentially to England. They sent their children to English schools. Their menfolk, clad in English uniforms, looked out from photographs that stood on drawing room tables. To say that is not to sneer. The family exercised considerable responsibility in that stretch of countryside. The various business ventures they had begun there gave employment to many. Their lands, known as the estate, were well run. Their business as far as possible went to the shopkeepers of that little town. Regularly Sunday by Sunday the elderly couple worshiped in Saint Mary's. As the bell rang they emerged, if it was a good morning, from a small gate in the walls surrounding the demesne. Crossing the road, they walked up the church driveway. If the weather was inclement, they used the car. Vast and shining and rather coachlike, it was not so much old as ageless. It moved with a stately authority and when the quiet elderly couple alighted, they did so with that slow dignity that their generation knew was also that of their majesties as they carried out the duties of a far-flung empire. If they had heard anyone say this of them, they would have rightly received it as a compliment. As they passed into the church porch, the menfolk stood around outside waiting for the bell to stop before taking their own places. All removed their hats in respect. Younger men and boys who were hatless nodded their heads and lifted their hands as if to pull at a real or imagined forelock.

Immediately inside the porch, the Captain and his wife turned to ascend the tiny circular stairs to the gallery. There was a curtain that divided the gallery in half. There, secluded by height and by the curtain, they both participated in and at the same time oversaw the community at worship. If there was Holy Communion, the rector would pause after the prayer of Humble Access. The congregation would remain kneeling. In the silence would be heard the creaking of the porch stairs. Slow, solemn treading came up the aisle. Children looked between their fingers. The Captain and his wife went forward to the altar rail and knelt to receive the sacrament. Only then did the rest of the community go forward to receive Holy Communion.

But that hierarchical little world, where the ladder between man and God had the most rigid gradations, also demanded responsibility in exchange for high status. The roof of the church was sound under the soft, penetrating Irish rain. The Captain would have seen to that when a roof was needed. The rectory was warm in winter with fuel from the Captain's estate. The church accounts were reviewed at the end of the year and he made any necessary contribution toward solvency. Such was the unified and, in a way, feudal world of church and manor house. There too in the pews was the gathered community—a doctor, a bank manager, a leading merchant, the steward of the estate, the teacher in the parish schoolhouse. Around them were the Church of Ireland families who farmed their acres along the valleys surrounding the town, among them my grandparents, uncles, aunts, and cousins.

To a small boy, the prayer desk where morning prayer was said looked large, distant, and exposed. Some years later while kneeling there I would learn the subtleties of religion and politics in that little world.

It was 1950 and I was in theology in Trinity College, Dublin. There came to Trinity a cry for help from Saint Mary's Castlecomer. The rector had been called away to a family death and someone was needed for Sunday morning. Because of my links with Castlecomer, I was sent on my eager way. Crisply cassocked and surpliced, I began morning prayer. As we moved through the service, I could see from where I knelt the Captain and his family in the gallery.

We said the Responses, coming finally to the petition that has provoked contention in the life of the Church of Ireland. For centuries it had been "O Lord save the King (or Queen)," to which the congregation had replied, "And mercifully hear us when we call upon Thee." The government of what had been now for some decades the "Republic of Ireland" had made what one might consider reasonable overtures to the Church of Ireland that its public petitions be changed from a prayer for the Queen or the King of England to one that reflected what had become the new political reality. A synod of the church had responded and after much debate, there had been produced a formula that sought to be both realistic yet reconciling. The prayer then read "O Lord guide and defend our rulers," to which the people gave the same ancient response "And mercifully hear us when we call upon Thee." This they could do of course with all sorts of mental reservations as to who their rulers really were, an administration in Dublin or King across the water. It was also a formula that might have, but did not, serve both north and south of the border even though in a world so divided politically the Church of Ireland had remained, and still remains, one.

What I did not realize that day as I knelt in Saint Mary's was that the congregation there had decided simply that the older petition would remain as it had always been. The rector would say, "O Lord save the King." I, not being the rector and being of a new generation who had grown up in the Republic, duly proclaimed the forbidden words

"O Lord guide and defend our rulers." It was followed by utter silence. It was a silence so deep that one became aware of the sounds of the countryside beyond the open windows. I remained kneeling, my mind racing, searching desperately for an explanation, until by some merciful intuition I realized what might be wrong. Hoping that my intuition was correct, I proclaimed with equal fervor, and with some desperation, "O Lord save the King." The answering voices came like a warm tide of affirmation as the congregation, especially its older parishioners, confessed their true allegiance.

Such political subtleties were then far in the future when I moved about the world of the farm in the mid and late 1930s. However there was nothing of subtlety or ambiguity in the message that a deeply pastoral church gave to its people.

It was an afternoon in late summer on the farm. Soon we would be returning to the city and to school. I was about nine. My grandmother, a prisoner of rheumatoid arthritis in her window chair, suddenly cried "The canon is coming." My aunt flew to the half door. Coming up the driveway was indeed the canon. He was pedaling slowly, his eyes to the ground. The hill up from the town had taken its toll. I suspected now that his thoughts were on such things as a cup of strong tea. In swift succession my aunt cast her apron in a corner, tidied her hair, put a kettle on the range, paused as if to collect herself, and went out to greet him. The kitchen darkened as they filled the low doorway. The canon entered, tall and imposing. There were greetings, my hand was shaken from a great height, my grandmother was greeted. Only then was the key taken from over the parlor door. That was in itself a measure of

the significance of that moment. The parlor was a forbidden land, attainable only on very special occasions. It
contained a huge table, a black leather couch, some chairs,
large yellowing photographs of my great grandparents,
and some old copies of the *Daily Sketch* for the year when
England had three kings—George V, Edward VIII, George
VI. As a special privilege, I was sometimes allowed to look
at the solemn events on those pages.

The canon and my aunt went to the parlor. I was sent
to find my mother who was feeding my baby brother, then
I was to go to the hay field and tell my grandfather and
uncles that the canon was in the house. I was unaware
that all this was an age-old and well-rehearsed liturgy
wherein all the players knew their parts. The canon knew
the men would be called in therefore he came near the
end of the working afternoon so that they would not lose
sunlit hours in the field. The men knew they had leeway
while my aunt got tea for the canon. This was a universe
of tradition and predictability. When I returned, my mother
and the baby were in the parlor, my aunt was preparing
tea, "tea" being hot apple pie and fresh griddle bread
with salty farm butter and jam. As if all was being coor-
dinated by an unseen director, tea was ready and laid on
the end table just as the men arrived from the fields. They
had thrown water on their faces and hands from the rain
barrel. Greetings were exchanged. Heads were bowed
while the canon said grace. He prayed for the family,
speaking loudly enough so that my grandmother in the
upper room could hear. My baby brother cried and was
quietly hushed, I suddenly remembered a simple lullaby
I was learning in poetry class.

> O! men from the fields!
> Come gently within,

Tread softly, softly,
O! men coming in.
Mavourneen is going
From me and from you,
Where Mary will fold him
With mantle of blue.

It was a moment for lifelong remembrance; a gathered family, the layers of generations, the sunlit fields, the richness of simple food, the church embodied in the tall figure at the table. For a child earth and heaven were for a moment one.

10. Conflict of Voices

It was significant that church and chapel were at opposite ends of the town. The Roman Catholic church, never called other than "the chapel" by Church of Ireland people, was much larger. For me Saint Mary's bell pealed gently, that of the Church of the Immaculate Conception boomed authoritatively. I loved the one and, I must confess, I feared the other. It had of course the eternal fascination of the totally forbidden. No Islamic prohibition on the outskirts of today's Mecca has more absolute authority than that prohibition had in our lives. As if both to warn and to tantalize, like the shimmering mirage in the desert that draws an unwary traveler from the right path, the blaze of what I now know to be the votive candle stand could be seen deep within the shadowed interior as one stood outside the huge doors. It is difficult to recall and almost impossible for us to understand today the immensity of that barrier. In the easy pluralism of North America, even to a lesser extent of today's Ireland, it is incomprehensible. To this very day, if I am involved in some event that entails worship in a large Roman Catholic church built on traditional lines, I am conscious of having come beyond some almost Himalayan range, of having entered a once forbidden country whose now familiar territory, demythologized by adult experience and a post–Vatican II world, still echoes half-remembered guilts and fears and longings, like the lost continents and valleys of Victorian fiction that echo with the cries of great beasts no longer part of the outside world.

On Sunday down the narrow country roads neighbors would answer the bells that called them respectively to mass or matins, benediction or evening prayer. The pony would be harnessed to the shafts of the trap. Cows newly milked would long since be back in the fields. Families saluted one another as they met or passed. In one great high trap drawn by a huge horse, I recall a boy my own age who had Down's Syndrome. It was severe as I only now realize. Even though hidden in the shelter of a large farm during the week, he would be dressed to join the family for Mass. It spoke to a child of the power of that Mass that this other boy, who both fascinated and alarmed me, probably because in age and coloring we were alike, was brought fully into the community for that strange mysterious rite carried out beyond my vision and chanted in ancient tongue.

The presence of the priest, the nun, and the friar were so common in Ireland before the Second World War that I can think of no parallel other than the legions of saffron-robed monks in the streets of a Burmese city. They were always visible. They signified a parallel world to the norm of lay life. They were in themselves a world intercepting the lay world. An odd element of that time was the fact that the actual person of the priest was sacrosanct. He carried on his person the Sacred Host. I can recall the absolute shock and horror registered in an Irish cinema when in the movie *San Francisco* Clark Gable struck Spencer Tracy who played a priest. When in the 1940s long lines outside theaters were nightly scenes in the towns, people would be standing sometimes for hours, frequently in pouring rain. The commissionaire, splendid in uniform, would go down the lines looking for priests who would immediately be brought into the theater and seated.

It is interesting that in much of the Anglo-Irish literature of the early and mid twentieth century, there is a good deal of anticlericalism. Much of it of course sprang from the effect of the rigid censorship imposed in the Republic on all writing. However I suspect also that much anticlericalism was born out of the resentment felt in the face of many rights and privileges not so much claimed as insensitively accepted. But even that anticlericalism was actually no more than a symptom of an incurable fascination with the church. It was as if the church's existence was necessary to provide an object sufficiently massive and impervious that could be railed against with magnificent and vitriolic eloquence but whose eternal resilience could be assumed without fear.

Agnosticism was seen by all Irish Christian traditions in those days as an eccentricity to be wondered at. Atheism, to the extent it was even conceivable, was the stuff of faraway benighted lands, including, incidentally, Europe. The only possible excuses for lack of faith were deemed to be invincible ignorance, insanity, or just possibly a demon whose name was Modernism. That ultimate enemy, it was felt, had been safely repelled from Irish shores.

So it was that the priest and the nun and the friar were absolutely interwoven with one's life. They shared a railway carriage or a bus. They bumped against one in the street. At a school sports meeting they were often the stewards, the sleeves of their habits rolled up on a sunny day, their fingers often brown with nicotine, their beards beaded with strong brown tea. The one consistent thing was that they were almost never seen alone. They appeared in pairs or in groups. This had the effect of their both mingling with the world yet being apart from it. I now realize that among the endless black-suited figures were tens of thousands of young seminarians. They were destined to become priests at altars from one end of the earth to the other. Ireland was then the great source of men for the Roman Catholic priesthood. It produced regiments of men and women for the churches and schools of five continents. In today's terms they were the Janissaries of the pre–Vatican II church—deeply conservative, fundamentalist in church doctrine, intensely loyal, totally dedicated. Somehow that implacable armor of conformity could not entirely hide a warmth and humor, a puckishness, a humanity that did much to disguise their utter single-mindedness and exclusivism where their church was concerned. Their continental brothers and sisters in priesthood or order frequently despaired of their naiveté but admired their devotion. One has only to recall the desperate loneliness of the aging Teilhard de Chardin in the New York clergy house where Irish priests found him at best incomprehensible and at worst heretical.

So it was that I became aware of two modes of spiritual authority in my experience as a child, one experienced directly, the other only by hearsay and observation. There seemed to be two modes in which the things of God were mediated and communicated in the community, both obviously hierarchical and both in their way authoritative. In both churches in the town the senior priest was called canon. Both were obviously of great significance in their respective congregations. I suspect that because of numbers there could not be the degree of intimacy between clergy and people in Immaculate Conception as there was in Saint Mary's. In the former there was a large staff of priests. In Saint Mary's there was the canon and the curate. The canon was permanent, the curate was transitory. To be visited by the curate was a pleasant diversion; to be visited by the canon was a serious occasion.

In my childhood the canon was a shy austere man, which made him seem remote in manner. But such was the immense trust between clergy and people in Ireland then that no mannerism or quirk of personality could ever break it. Small talker or not, reserved or hearty, the canon was always given a warm welcome. He in his turn, in spite of the rigidly graded social universe of the Irish countryside, would have been hurt and dismayed if anyone had imputed that in its time of need, the humblest home would not have gotten from him his utmost pastoral care. It undoubtedly would have.

There tended, however, to be a circle in which the Church of Ireland rector moved in a community. It was not in any sense a question of snobbery. It was merely the way things were in an older society. Sometimes bonds would be formed by there being the shared world of the same university. There might be the recollection of war service or, further back, boarding school. All such things tended to form a network of friendships. As well the sprinkling of professionals in any small Irish town tended to get to know each other if for no other reason than their mutual involvement in the lives of individuals and families who from time to time needed guidance or assistance in their affairs. Thus the clergy, the doctor, the lawyer, the schoolteacher, the leading merchants, the local landowning families, all tended to form social links and relationships.

Because of warm friendliness shown to me as a child, I recall a charmingly eccentric household of two sisters and a brother. They had, as they would have said in those days, "connections" in Dublin. They lived in the town square and had a maid. They rarely ventured out, sending for their needs to the various shops. Their brother, who had no visible means of support and therefore was in the exalted position, as they would have said, of having money, paraded everyday sporting a walking stick and colorful tweeds, conferring hearty salutations on all whom he encountered. The locals, perceiving him to be a man of obvious if quaint authority who spoke with an accent somewhere between the suburbs of Dublin and a British officers' mess, accorded him respect mingled with patient and charitable hilarity.

The remaining family who moved in the orbit of the rectory was an Anglo-Irish family with British Army connections. A high wall, a gravel driveway, and a motorcar were sufficient to place them apart. Yet even here the social distinctions were infinitely subtle. Somehow one saw even as a child that, though the owner bore the same army rank as the Captain in the Big House, the families were somehow not quite on the same level. For all I know, the reality may have been merely a difference of regiment.

Revolving at some subtly lower level came my family and the various friends who from time to time moved in and out of our lives from neighboring farms. My mother's grandfather had come over from Yorkshire to be steward on the surrounding estate. At some point the family had acquired their own farmlands so the immediate connection was broken, while a relationship of remembered mutual affection and respect remained.

Thus did our lives impinge on that of the rectory and its life on ours. The social compact in which we all lived was a subtle blend of unity and divisions, links and barriers. The word *subtle* hints at its being contrived, but it was rather the result of a convoluted history that had placed together on that little island a small landowning class for whom England was spiritual home, not to mention the source of many pensions, and a mildly prosperous farming class who with fierce pride saw their diminishing links with the British empire as giving their Church of Ireland faith a significance beyond their numbers in the face of a huge Roman Catholic majority. This latter faith was then largely that of a world of peasant folk, workers, and small farm holders who held to it with utter loyalty. Not many years later all that would change as Roman Catholic higher education would begin to produce a new generation of men and women to enter the professions and change the face of Irish public life.

Across those different worlds was woven a web of personal friendships. Always there would be ready cooperation at such times as harvesting, families helping each other irrespective of creed. There was only one prohibition and that was absolute. It was mixed marriage. It stood as a wall between those little worlds, and against its implacable stone face families were often broken by fear and despair.

It was largely because of the social and religious erosion threatened by mixed marriage that the Church of Ireland community, in spite of any lines of social distinction operating within it, was never in doubt that it was indeed a community. It saw itself essentially as a ghetto, without the social impetus and physical limitations that sometimes go with that state. Even in the cities, it was not so much a matter of where Church of Ireland people lived as how they lived. Much lifestyle was defined in contrast to Roman Catholic mores. If "they" did something, "we" did not. If "they" went to certain places, "we" did not. "They" played hurling and Gaelic football. "We" played English rugby, cricket, and field hockey. To make life even more confusing, by the time my generation was beginning to socialize in the upper teen years, some of "them" were playing "our" games.

Above all, the use of Sunday still marked a day of distinction. For the Roman Catholic community, as long as one went "to hear Mass" (as the saying went), the rest of the day was free for celebration. Public games, movies were popular. For us Sunday retained well into the twentieth century what we now tend to think of as only the shape of the nineteenth. Morning Sunday school at ten was followed by Morning Prayer at eleven. Afternoon "childrens' service" came at three. For those of us in the choir, Evensong was at seven, and following that came Boys and Girls Brigade Bible class at half past eight. It's hard to believe that most of my contemporaries in the community took the sequence absolutely for granted. The reason I suspect was that it was, of course, universal. Everybody else whom one knew was involved in the same stream. As we all grew older, we would again meet at the numerous parish dances in the halls of the churches. It was presumed that we would marry among the faces and voices known since childhood. Beyond that there was the hope that we would find employment in the enterprises of Church of Ireland businessmen. These, while seeming to welcome the youth of their church as employees, frequently used the interdependence of the ghetto to keep salaries low. Thus, though they neither realized it nor intended it, they inadvertently encouraged the emigration of many who would otherwise have enriched and strengthened their own community.

11. A Song Overheard

From where I stood at the open window, I looked out over the roofs of north Dublin. The hostel housing those of us who were doing theology in Trinity College stood in the middle of what had been referred to as the most noble slum in Europe. Street after street was bounded by once magnificent Georgian houses that had by then decomposed into cavernous open doors, smashed windows, garbage-lined sidewalks, and an all-pervading odor. That sea of poverty and despair had within it islands of what was probably seen as institutionalized opulence but which was certainly, at least in the case of our hostel, scrubbed austerity.

The year was 1950. In the great square over to my right were the buildings where James Joyce sat at school not that many years ago, a student absorbing the images that in later years were to paint such devastating portraits of that little world. On that November evening the smoke of fireplaces, railway engines, and double-decker buses was mingling with a fog coming in from the Irish sea. The sky was overcast with the last of a watery sunset etched along the western line of the suburbs. But I was not there to watch the sunset. The reason the window was open was so that I could hear the sound that was coming from the center of the city. The reason for the sound had been announced in all the papers. There had been brought to Ireland a very sacred relic, the right arm of Saint Francis Xavier. Tonight it was to be on public display, and it would be the focus of evening devotions in one of the huge city churches.

The response was overwhelming. All around the church traffic was clogged. Men and women were kneeling in the wet streets. The church was long since packed. The sound of the chanting within was picked up by those outside. It lifted on the evening air and moved across the city. It overwhelmed the noise of traffic. Rising and falling, it voiced a great tide of emotion that was neither joy nor sorrow but an ecstacy beyond both, a passion beyond explanation, a mystery beyond all theology.

I now realize that while I may have lived in a Protestantism that sometimes saw itself as a ghetto, albeit a comfortable and influential one, we all in reality inhabited a world I would once have called Catholic but now would rather call mystical. In that little world of long ago, I would not have been able to make that distinction. That would come later.

Our family name was one naturally assumed to be Roman Catholic. Our being other seemed to be an anomaly. My great grandfather with his wife and children had changed sometime in the mid to late nineteenth century. I've never been able to find the precise time or reason. All I know is that it was not a mixed marriage. It is a measure of the hold history has on us all that even as I write this now more than a century and a quarter later, my hope is that they did not have to change as many did in the terrible years of the famine, desperately responding to some well-meaning but overzealous Protestant soup kitchen that offered them nourishment for their hungry children if they converted.

Long generations of West Cork peasant mingled in my

parents with English Yorkshire farming stock. On my father's side the family in the remote past had a history of petty piracy and smuggling among the wild and vicious tidal inlets of West Cork and South Kerry. I can remember a moment of very special pride. As one of a group of small boys in the Boys Brigade, I sailed one day to Shirken Island off the coast of Cork. Beaching the boat, we ran across the rough grasses, bent against the ceaseless Atlantic wind, and saw the ruined walls of an abbey built by an ancestor of mine in the fifteenth century. It was a moment of rich realization of oneself as the possessor of a long story, whatever its shades of kindness and cruelty, acquisition or generosity, good or evil.

I was afraid at first to step over a low part of the fallen outer wall, but I finally did. I moved in a few steps through the overgrown uneven ground. I looked out through the last remaining window sockets to where the white clouds scudded across the cold blue sky. I stood there for a moment, a soul brought home in a child's body, until a shout and a companion's push ended the intersection of time and timelessness, outer existence and inner journey.

In so many ways, the Catholic world that surrounded our official Protestantism called one. There were, of course, strong efforts made at conversion. It was done without apology, often in such places as hospital wards where some lonely soul's defenses were low and a relationship had formed with a chaplain or a nursing sister. I suspect in retrospect that while we saw it as villainy and betrayal, they did it with the very best of intentions for the welfare of an eternal soul. "Nulla salvus ex ecclesia" was as much a reality in that Ireland as gravity in a Newtonian universe.

The irony was that the unconscious and implicit call of

the quality I thought of then as Catholic was strong in itself, stronger, as a matter of fact, and more attractive than the institutional church that seemed to embody it. It seemed to be something quite beyond institutionalized religion, something undefinable that seemed then to make it as natural to be Roman Catholic in Ireland as it is to be Hindu in India; a totality, a web of atmosphere, memory, mythology, national character, language, history. A moment of particular poignancy comes to mind.

It was 1943 and from our boarding school we were driven over the Knockmealdown Mountains into the lowlands of Tipperary to play cricket against Rockwell College, a school run by one of the church orders. I realize now that the order was setting out to produce the first generation of a Roman Catholic professional class in Ireland, hence the anomaly at that time of a Roman Catholic school playing the English game of cricket. After the game we had supper in the school. The buildings awed us. The place seemed at least half a dozen times the size of our school.

At the end of the meal one of the staff suggested an impromptu concert. One of their senior boys, in a voice about to possess that haunting Irish-tenor quality, sang "The Hills of Donegal." As he did, the pure voice echoed in the tiled and stained-glass vaulting of the hall. I recall an intense longing to be able to identify in that total way with the country of my birth instead of feeling sometimes a hybrid of mingled loyalties.

Yet, in the same boarding school to which we returned that evening, a school called Midleton College, just on the edge of a small town of the same name in the eastern pasturelands of County Cork, I was already learning something that one day would help to bring together the disparate elements of identity I was seeking. It was an implicit learning, given to me by the gifts of two very different teachers.

Andrew MacBride communicated to us his great love of music, revealing music to us as a means for setting the mind free to journey into landscapes within oneself. Every Sunday evening of term the whole school would assemble for a recorded recital of classical music. Very short notes would be read before each recording. I now realize that he had the wisdom to include just enough "pop" classics like Ravel's "Bolero" and Rimsky Korsakov's "Flight of the Bumblebee" to engage our sometimes unwilling ears.

There were a few simple rules about these forty-five-minute-long sessions. You could not do any homework, nor could you talk. You could write a letter home. You could, as a few of us discovered, do something else. You could agree with someone else to write down what was going through your mind as you listened to the music, then compare notes after the recital about the images each had written down.

I realize now that this primitive, youthful inner voyaging was a door opening early to landscapes that would stretch far into the future and become richer with time. We were beginning to see one thing as another, to discover language for the elusive, for things felt, imagined, dreamed. We were learning to capture the fleeting images of transient worlds of fantasy.

The other master was Mr. Power. His nickname, not to his face of course, was "Paddy." There was an element of irony in that because there was about him something of the foreign and the exotic. He was a slim, black-haired man with a delicate, fine-boned face. He embodied that physical type in Ireland that reminds you that the crews of many Armada ships sought refuge in Ireland's west coast harbors as their fleet was overcome by the terrible weather after Drake had savaged them in the Channel. He taught us Gaelic and English literature. He himself could also speak Spanish. He had a gentle disposition, a subtle sense of humor that was never hurtful, and a magnificent flair for the dramatic. He taught us to love language both Gaelic and English, for its own sake. He taught us to recite aloud both Irish poetry (in Gaelic) and Shakespearean soliloquies. By doing so he taught us, without ever having to say it explicitly, that each possessed its natural and rightful honor and that each was capable of becoming the bearer of beauty and the expression of valuable truths.

I was fortunate to encounter him. He fostered the love of Gaelic as a language. All of us had to learn it as the official policy of a Republic. Few liked it. I loved it. It opened doors to a rich northern mythology. It gave one access to poetry deeply mystical. It was the womb that fed Yeats and Synge and that, even though they wrote in English, formed their rich cadences and furnished them with their most vivid images and themes.

Many Gaelic poets of the seventeenth and eighteenth centuries had been translated into English by nineteenth-century Irish and Anglo-Irish writers. The patriotic images and themes of these poems would later feed the revolutionary fervor of the early twentieth century. However, since a new generation was growing up at a time when a young state was insisting on the revival of the Gaelic language, killed by English decree from the late seventeenth century on, we were to discover much Irish poetry in the original language.

To do so was to discover a poetry as delicate and mystical as at other times it could be earthy and violent.

The spectrum showed clearly the twin heroes of early Celtic culture, the warrior and the poet. Ultimate heroism was to be both. In 1916 the ancient romantic image would be embodied in Patrick Pearse amid the rubble of the general Post Office in Dublin, eventually taking to the firing squad at one and the same time a sensitive poet, a revolutionary soldier, a politician idealistic almost to the point of unreality.

I realize now that the thread that bound such poetry together was its natural assumption that all things are sacred. This laid an indelible foundation, forming a reality where spirituality and life could never be seen apart. The divine did not hover above experienced reality but indwelt it. I had without knowing it begun to realize that while the Star of the Magi high above the town has its significance as guide and symbol, real significance is found in the manger of the mundane, the ordinary, the daily experienced event. Later this would form for me a unified world where nature, the city, relationships, imagination, sexuality, and art would all be the natural abode of spirituality, all serving as the hiding places of God.

The giant of Anglo-Irish poetry is W. B. Yeats. To live within his poetry, to have stood at Inisfree and heard "lake water lapping with low sounds by the shore"; to have stood in South Donegal near the Rosses, envisaging the king of the fairy hosts as "on a bridge of white mist Columcille he crosses, on his stately journeys from Slieve League to Rosses"; all that was to engender a deep mystical sense of the created order as laden and shimmering with the presence of the sacred. At that time a sense of a divinized creation was not consciously linked with the neat and ordered questions and answers in the Catechism of the Book of Common Prayer then being learned by rote. But slowly, and now from the vantage of time clearly recognized, links were forming between a youthful pantheism and an embryonically Trinitarian faith.

One poet above all still sings for me. He wrote in that highly romantic, violent, and tragic moment of literary revival and political revolution that saw the formation of the Abbey Theater, the early poetry of Yeats, and the abortive rebellion of 1916. His name was Joseph Mary Plunkett and he suffered the death penalty for his involvement.

> I see his blood upon the rose
> And in the stars the glory of his eyes.
> His body gleams amid eternal snows,
> His tears fall from the skies.
>
> I see his face in every flower;
> The thunder and the singing of the birds
> Are but his voice, and carven by his power
> Rocks are his written words.
>
> All pathways by his feet are worn,
> His strong heart stirs the ever-beating sea,
> His crown of thorns is twined with every thorn,
> His Cross is every tree.

12. A Story Discovered

Why then did I not in a spiritual sense go home, that is, become Roman Catholic? How can one give an answer? I suspect that in a matter as complex and as sensitive as the human spiritual journey, there are very few answers of a simple and precise kind. Why does one fall in love? And why with this person rather than that? Why does one give one's loyalty to this cause or that? One cannot answer. One tries to respond, to reflect on the why, to unravel the pattern, knowing even then that threads will remain unnoticed in the richness of the design.

For one thing, I came to realize the amazing and often unrealized paradox about Ireland, that the vast majority of those who expressed its longing for political freedom, who wrote its loveliest poetry and its greatest plays and novels, who translated its half-lost early Gaelic language and rescued it from oblivion, were not Roman Catholic. I remember the moments in the Abbey Theater when this paradox came home to me, once when watching Sean O'Casey's *The Plough and the Stars* and again while watching Yeats's *The Countess Kathleen*. I remember as a student the immense liberation this realization gave.

In the next few years there were to be other moments of such discovery and liberation. Those were the immediate postwar years of the late forties and fifties. For decades Ireland had been an island in every sense, its long centuries of outreach to Europe a twelve hundred-year memory idealized and romanticized in Christian history. Suddenly there were among us in university men and women from other countries whose government grants for service in the war were now making it possible for them to return to university. Among them were men and women who had experienced another Anglicanism, richer in liturgical color and symbol, highly sacramental. Among us too came a then unknown Russian Orthodox priest named Anthony Bloom embodying hitherto unimagined horizons of Orthodox spirituality. Raymond Raynes, Prior of the Community of the Resurrection in Mirfield, Yorkshire, would also visit. Gaunt, eyes sunken, soft voiced, sitting in university rooms speaking of things we had never realized were ours as Anglicans—the Blessed Sacrament, Mary, confession, a host of saints other than the great Celtic figures we had long taken for granted. The voice of Stephen Neill, mellifluous, English, cosmopolitan, at home in Lambeth, Bangalore, New York, Australia, the Caribbean, spoke of eighteenth and nineteenth-century mission in all its rich tapestry of Evangelical and Catholic Anglicanism.

All were part of the same liberating process. I could possess what I had thought belonged only to others. The mysticism, the earthiness, the sacramentality were all possible in my own spiritual family now that I had been introduced to its diversity and treasures.

Meanwhile in the daily experience of doing theology in Trinity College I came to realize that at the heart of the tradition given to me by home and church and society there lay intertwined a story and a secret. To be precise, there were two stories, one of which was my gift from Judaism. Both are stories about God. Indeed it may be more true to say that both are stories told by God about himself.

The first and older story is that God is the Creator of

and the Dweller within all that is, and through his involvement with a People, becomes involved with humanity. The second and newer story is that God entered into a woman's womb, thus entering our very flesh and all human experience.

Within these two stories there lies, as I discovered, a secret corollary. It says that human life reaches the source of deepest meaning to the extent that we develop a sense of seeing the invisible in and through the visible, of touching the intangible in and through the tangible.

"No man" claims the writer of scripture "hath seen God at any time." However, no sooner has scripture stated this than it introduces us to the endless sequence of men and women who do see God. Perhaps one should say that they see God as Crusoe saw the marks of another human footprint in the sand of his hitherto solitary island. So the footprint of the passing of God is discerned in daily experience, in the events of private and public history, in the glory and terror of nature, and in the mystery and complexity of human encounter and relationship.

In classes in a parish school, later in boarding school, I would come upon the stories themselves, stories of encounter between human beings and God. Eve in the garden of the newly born world, Noah in his drowning valley, Abraham homesick for Ur, Jacob tossing in nightmare at Bethel, Moses in the desert, Isaiah's vision of great wings, Mary tremulous before her angel, Jesus half naked in the Jordan, Paul on the Damascus road, John grown old on Patmos. With all of them, the ordinary was seen as signifying more than itself. Thus for Amos a plumb line became an image of justice and integrity. Hosea agonized over his failed marriage and conceived the depths of God's love for a People. Jesus watched a woman searching for a coin and saw an image of the Kingdom of Heaven. These I would come to know, not realizing that mine would be the last generation for whom these things would be taught and learned as normally as mathematics, history, poetry, or gymnastics.

The common attribute of so many lives in the Bible is this ability to see signs. The simple word *sign* gives us the word *significance* and that is essentially the quest I speak of, the discerning of significance in daily experience. Among the few expressions of exasperation we hear from our Lord are those in which he expresses regret at the inability of some to see signs of God's activity in the things happening around them.

Thus it is that a Babylonian storyteller looked at the sky and the Euphrates and the desert and, seeing them as signs of One beyond and above them, gave us the majesty of the first chapter of Genesis. In journeying from Ur to Canaan Abraham knew himself as not merely moving from one context to another for his business enterprises. He answered a call that had consequence and meaning. For Noah the rising waters of his disintegrating world were not merely the result of ecological imbalance. He was aware that he had been called toward a future made possible only if men and women acted faithfully in apocalypse. To Jacob, as to many in the Bible, a dream was not merely a manifestation of overtiredness or hypertension. It was a message from heaven to earth, an angel of warning or encouragement or affirmation. For Moses a burning bush called for a turning aside. Bushes burn almost routinely for us all, yet it is our capacity to see faces in the flames and voices in the fire that makes the moment more than routine and therefore pregnant with possibility. For a fleeing people, survival in the mud flats and tidal reaches of a great river delta was more than a convenient environmental happenstance. It became a never-to-be-forgotten sign of a destiny given them by God. For Wise Men, a star was more than an item of astronomical data. It became a sign of birth and change and a new age. For Jesus, coins and sheep and fishes and weddings, seeds, a door, a tree, a widow, a conversation, a loaf of bread, a glass of wine, a candle, a presuming guest at a dinner party, a vial of ointment, even his own death; all were more than object, incident, event, experience. All were made into signs and parables and insights so vivid that for two millennia they became the outriders of a kingdom, the symbols enabling us to express the inexpressible, lights that guide us in our fearful voyaging across the terrible crystal seas of mystery that, as Saint John tells us, lie between our earthbound humanity and the throne of God.

Thus scripture became for me a womb of endless signs, an admonition to seek their meanings for myself. It was above all to me a finger pointing to the ordinary as the place of the divine dwelling, pointing to Bethlehem rather than to Rome or Athens, to a peasant girl rather than to a queen, to a child rather than an emperor. One might add in passing that, for those who perceive, Bethelehem becomes both Rome and Athens, the peasant girl is revealed as queen, and the child becomes king. The insignificant has assumed significance, the mundane become sign.

Some years would pass before I fully ventured on the highway that runs from the New Testament to my own time. Passing by the caves of the desert fathers of the fourth century, past the stone oratories built against sixth-century Atlantic gales, sweeping through lovely places such as Iona and Lindisfarne, through busy places like Assisi and Chichester and Norwich, that highway is of course the Way of the Saints and a crowded and varied human procession traffics along its length.

When I came to the Saints I was made aware of them as men and women who lived very much in reality, who had frequently acted in it with something less than perfection, yet whose peculiar significance and fascination lay in the fact that, while occupying what we call reality, they were constantly aware of another reality. Francis looked back at a leper and saw Christ. Ignatius Loyola felt death pass him in a cannonball's flight and it became to him a vocation that brought into existence the Jesuits. Patrick plucked a tiny plant and saw the Eternal Trinity. Julian of Norwich held a hazelnut in her dreaming hand and saw the universe in the hand of a God who was Maker, Lover, Keeper. On and on they go, seeing one thing as another, dismissed as mad by their friends, heretical by churchmen, subversive by kings.

Madness, heresy, subversion—there are of course always those possibilities in seeing signs. There exists as attractive a succession of signs between earth and hell as between earth and heaven. Monsters in human form have rested their case on a call from God in some sign. In the cymbals of Wagner's music Adolf Hitler heard the howling of the Norse gods calling for the world's terrible cleansing at his own hands. Josef Stalin walked toward the altar of Orthodox priesthood, only to eventually become a high priest of unrestrained butchery. Lesser in iniquity, Constantine saw a night-sky cloud formation as a Cross and became at one and the same time Christian hero and anti-Semite.

Where lies the boundary between sainthood and

psychosis, between divine call, chemical imbalance, demonic possession? Given enough lust for the secular and the mechanistic, we can effectively dissect a Paul, a Pascal, a Theresa, a Bonhoeffer, earnestly attaching our psychological labels and assigning each to his or her medically defined category. Only when we walk away from the cell to which we have assigned them and look back do we see a strange light blazing underneath the locked door, making us, if we are wise, fall on our knees.

The work of the early Celtic monks shows in artistic images what I have tried to express in words. On many an afternoon I read or wrote in the Long Room of the library in Trinity College. At the halfway point of this long, high, book-lined gallery there was a simple glass case. Inside it lay the Book of Kells. It is regarded by some as the most magnificent manuscript in the world. It is a copy of the Four Gospels in Latin, a copy made in the monastery of Kells in County Meath in Ireland about A.D. 800.

It is the magnificent illuminations on the ancient vellum that communicate something of the way in which Celtic spirituality looked at the world. To look down at the ancient page opened for that particular day is to see first perhaps only a single letter, huge, vivid, elaborately fashioned. There may be no more than one or two words on the page beginning a gospel or a chapter. But around these two words there spills onto the parchment a flood of the most intricate and detailed designs one can conceive. As one looks, one finds level after level of further microscopic design.

What one is looking at in the Book of Kells is an image of reality seen as a kind of deep shimmering well. As with a well, one's sight can remain on the surface or the eyes

can sink downward in the bottomless depths. The art calls
one to look through each level to another.

In that word *through* lies, for me, the common treasure
of Celtic spirituality. It is, as I have tried to express, a
repeated theme in the Old Testament and with Jesus of
Nazareth. To look, not merely at reality but through reality,
is the secret of spiritual experience, the avenue to the
presence of the holy, the door between the worlds.

That secret of the spirit is, of course, not the sole
prerogative of Celtic spirituality. Because it is forever un-
quenchable, it has flared like a burning bush in Western
spirituality, even in ages when Western eyes since the
seventeenth century were becoming so mesmerized by
physical reality that they seemed incapable any longer of
looking through it to that which lay hidden and which
called beyond it. George Herbert, to name but one, is the
authentic voice of that spirituality when he writes.

> A man that looks on glasse,
> On it may stay his eye;
> Or if he pleaseth, through it passe,
> And then the heav'n espie.

Thus it was that during those university years I came to
realize that those elements of beauty and mystery that
existed as images about me and sounded as voices within
me were not necessarily solely the treasure and heritage
of one particular Christian tradition. They were already
mine by virtue of where I was. All this was not a cerebrally
appropriated theological system, still less a denomina-
tional monopoly. Thus, in the words of Saint Patrick's
Breastplate, itself among the great expressions of Celtic
spirituality, I could not only sing "I bind unto myself today / The Strong name of the Trinity" but I could also

claim as mine a spirituality rich in its sense of the earth, articulate in story, passionate in its living, which continually pierced the visible and tangible world around me, revealing glimpses of an elusive and haunting glory.

Such a glimpse was given in childhood on a late Sunday afternoon in Summertime. In the front pews of the vast and otherwise empty church we children were being addressed by a young priest, a person I would know in later life and recognize as sensitive and imaginative. We were about to sing a hymn. He told us to look up. Obediently we gazed into the great vault above the chancel. It was resplendent with angels and stars and trumpets and clouds. He told us that if we sang very loudly the stars would shine more brightly. Several years were to pass finding at least one child looking up with increasing but reluctant doubt until I came to a sad but triumphant certainty that they did not. Now I realize after much time that he was telling us a truth greater than the chipped paint and the mediocre art of that long-ago ceiling. I realize that the stars did most certainly and most gloriously shine as they will always shine when the child within me sings the praise of God.

13. Journey to Maturity

At the top of a hill, in a spacious square surrounded by Georgian mansions, in the heart of the Dublin slums, stood the Divinity Hostel. It housed men studying for ordination in Trinity College. It fed us and sheltered us for the modest sum of thirteen guineas, then about fifty dollars, per term, providing what today would be called "community." Though we did not fully realize it, it also provided us with the rare opportunity of living, eating, conversing, praying, studying, and worshiping with a genuinely saintly man. His name was Michael Lloyd Ferrar.

He was a solitary man, pathetically shy, formidably well-read, highly disciplined, deeply spiritual. All of these things he communicated to us. At that time youth, self-centeredness, insensitivity, and ignorance armored us against realizing fully the loveliness of his spirit. Only in time, like the richest and best wine, would his spirit become apparent to many of us in our later years, we being by that time spread across the world, myself in Canada.

Michael Ferrar linked my isolated Irish Christianity with the mysticism of Eastern Orthodoxy, a world my ancestors had encountered along the Danube nearly eleven hundred years previously, long before its break from old Rome. He taught me the nighttime power of the ancient monastic service called Compline to calm fears. He taught me that when the Psalmist spoke of "secret" sins, he did not mean those that a man knows of in himself but, precisely the opposite, it means those things hidden from a man about himself. Thus he taught me of the unconscious by way of the poetry of the fourth century B.C. He told me also, standing together outside the door of the chapel, that I must pack a bag and go home because my father was seriously ill. In doing so, I now realize that he also communicated to me, without ever saying so, that he had become the first of the fathers who would be given to me for this particular journey.

The memory of the journey itself is shrouded in night. The train pulled out of Kingsbridge Station at some very late hour. Until the morning I occupied a small, dimly lit compartment from which I could escape only by moving out into the cold lurching corridor and gazing toward the dark countryside rushing past. To sleep was also to escape, but it was never for very long. A particularly strong shudder of the train would jerk me awake, recalling me to anxiety and fear. At intervals in this misery and restlessness, I would doggedly read a few more paragraphs from a biography of William Temple, onetime archbishop of Canterbury. I realize now that bringing it with me was an unconscious attempt to pretend that there was a normal continuity between this night and those that had preceded it. Insisting on normality and continuity, my mind was refusing to accept the enormity of what at some level I knew to be near.

There remains only a succession of mental images, a reel of film full of the sudden scene changes of old primitive movies. My father greeting me in his hospital bed with infinite weariness, his eyes seeking me but finding great difficulty in remaining engaged with mine. A doctor, to me elderly, distant, totally devoid of feeling, telling me of the malignancy, the operation that had been necessary, the strain on my father's heart, the possibility that he might not recover.

There is an evening memory of going to a familiar rectory, the house I had always known beside the parish church, opening the heavy iron gate at the end of the graveled driveway, walking up through the sweet-smelling shrubbery of early summertime, being received into a book-lined study, and talking until long past midnight with one who was given to me as yet another father and who walked home with me in the sleeping city.

As I stood beside the hospital bed, I saw my father's hands were outside the bedclothes, white, blue veined, restless. He insisted I give him some coins from the little table. I did so and he handled a florin piece, the symbol of the leaping salmon on it turning again and again in his hands. He was confused. I realized that he was distressed because he thought there were two coins and was trying to separate them. Tears of frustration came to his eyes. I realized that he was moving farther from me. My younger brothers had gone home. I left, my mother wishing to stay.

My father had been moved to another ward. In later years I would come to know so well this quietly programmed progression of receding mortality as I stood with other families in faraway hospitals. Now each stage was mystifying, its details vivid and arresting like a play never before seen. My father was on his side in the bed, his body curled as if in deep sleep, his breathing labored, the sound harsh and loud in the silent room. The hours slipped by, measuring the gradual occupation of the room by a terrible intruder. A sudden spasm of obvious distress and struggle brought an oxygen unit. The quiet hiss became the background to the whispered attempts at conversation between my mother and myself.

The door opened and the canon came in. In physical stature he was a small man. He came to us as a giant of assurance, care, dependability. We knew he could not vanquish this greatest of enemies in our family life. All we knew was that his presence brought something totally beyond definition but of infinite value. He was still with us when there was a sudden change in the rhythm of my father's breathing, a succession of quiet gasps, each one weaker than the last, then silence. Only the sound of the oxygen tank broke the silence, its sibilant consistency mocking the poor lurchings of our human breath giving itself to tears.

For a moment I was conscious of an immense sense of mystery. With part of my mind I knew that my father had died. Yet in those first moments disbelief challenged the knowledge. I was aware of a new quality of stillness. I had never seen sleep like that. I became aware of the canon saying the prayers of commendation as he stood beside us. I was conscious of a sudden image of a vast vaulted universe, splendid with planetary systems and wheeling galaxies, into which my father had stepped and among which he began to journey. As we stood together in the timeless way of families experiencing this dark visitation, we were released from immobility by the canon's gentle invitation to come home and rest. There was a last silent kiss to my father's still face and then we went, the small figure of the canon shepherding us forward, quietly playing the priestly role of father.

In that moment it was given to me to glimpse something of the reality of priesthood and to discern some small facet of its eternal validity and worth in the human journey.

14. The Courts of the Lord

In ancient Greece there stood the labyrinth by which men came to their encounter with the terrible Minotaur. In the formal gardens of the sixteenth and seventeenth centuries there stood the maze in which men and women reflected or dallied and in which children acted out fears of being lost in reassuring afternoon sunlight.

Both are images of the convoluted ways by which we all come to the partial understandings of our journey. I have been trying to trace some paths by which I came to what I will call intimations of Divine Immanence. I speak of an instinct, a hunch, a suspicion that the divine is somehow hidden in the stuff of human experience; that the divine enters again and again through the side doors of the stages of our experience, flitting at the edge of our vision, wanting to be seen and recognized, rarely showing itself center stage in high drama, speaking quietly its sometimes single line that, if we but hear it, may alert us to the true identity of the voice. Yet when we look, the figure has vanished.

Because I am a Christian, it is naturally the symbols of Christian tradition that for me serve to give face and name to this sense of the Divine Immanence. For the Christian the ultimate moment of that immanence is the interfacing of the Divine and the human in Jesus Christ.

However I am fully aware that such things may be approached only behind the screens of metaphor, simile, image, analogy, parable, dream, story. I am aware that for millennia Jews, perceiving this mystery, have refused, even as they read their sacred scrolls, to utter the Holy Name.

I am aware that even when in Jesus Christ the Divine glory shares my very flesh as brother, sucks at the breast, and dies my human death, I still encounter a mystery that, however familiar it may become in sacrament, gospel, or worship, is forever a fearful thing even though the matter of its fearfulness be an unbounded love. Jesus my brother is, in the same moment of intimacy, also for me the Christ. Hand in hand go familiarity and awe. The simplicity of the stable brings even kings to their knees even though there lies therein a human child. One is forever Mr. Rat and Mr. Mole in Kenneth Graham's *Wind in the Willows*, hearing the distant piping of Pan, being drawn irresistably toward it, rowing their tiny boat up the great river to the sacred grove, knowing the tightening of the throat that is love yet at the same time the lassitiude of the limbs that is fear.

I am trying to name the way in which for me human experience is invaded by another mode of reality. Perhaps invasion is too strong a word. It might be more true to speak of a gentle interpenetration. Yet even as I seek the right term, I know that the reality is both. There are times when human experience is invaded with power and undeniable demand. Invitation is not the only mode by which we are addressed, giving us unhurried time for reflection about our response. There are also moments of thundering proclamation from the whirlwind of human events to which we can offer nothing other than prostration.

It may well be that for another, that which invites or invades will not be named by the language of faith though it share its source and, in its own way, becomes grace to us. In music a piece such as "Andante Cantabile" may be what I have called a gentle interpenetration of music and listener. Beethoven in full surge is thundering proclamation to which the listener can only bow down.

Because of the strong bonds between church and society in the Ireland of my childhood, all experience came to me mediated by the church. If that is to any degree an exaggeration of memory, it is certainly true that no aspect of life was for a moment thought of as outside the divine realm symbolized by Sacrament, Word, and Sanctuary. That fact did not of course prevent the realization that the God for whom Altar and Book exist was not contained within these things. This God spoke in the wind and the waves, the trees and the fields, had entered time in a woman's womb yet was also Lord over time, bisecting it by Resurrection, ruling both womb and universe with equal majesty.

The institutional church is a thing of grime and glory. Because it is composed of human beings, it is riddled with all the mixed baggage we humans drag with us on our groping journey. As an institution it can display all that dark side of humanity each of us knows so well in ourselves.

But there are reasons why that will never be the end of the story. The first is that the church, in a way that often confounds its harshest critics, brings to birth great souls who blaze like lights in the shadows of history, whose loveliness and courage and selflessness radiate not only into the darkest and most unattractive corners of the church's life, but also into a world distrustful of yet desperately longing for goodness.

The second reason is that within the life of any Christian community there are daily actions and decisions and sacrifices carried out by seemingly ordinary people living seemingly humdrum lives that show them to be spiritual giants. Last and perhaps most inexplicable of all is the fact that there lives within the life of the church, yet also above and beyond it, a power that does not allow it to forget the incalculable cost paid in suffering to give it birth and continued life. Christians have their own language for this power, calling it Holy Spirit, recognizing that it has shown itself time and time again to be a creative and reforming reality.

I realize the church of which I was a child had a love affair with the past that was both its weakness and its strength. On more than one occasion I have suggested that this fascination with the past was a characteristic of a whole people rather than of a particular institution. But even if a love affair with the past has its costs, it also offers many treasures, among them a sense of long tradition and a many-leveled story.

Nowhere is this seen more clearly than in the way in which late twentieth-century Christians are turning home toward the eucharistic meal as the center of their spiritual life, thus defining themselves as a community of faith within the human family, one that eats the sacred meal and reads and tells the sacred story. To recover that sense of faith community is also to recapture an older term— "the communion of Saints," that vast company of those who have believed in every age.

By discovering this we gain access to the creativity and devotion of all who have formed the community before us. Thus are we released to give thanks for stone placed on stone by other hands, design formed within design by other eyes, color blended with color in shining stained glass or tapestry weave, language so expressive as to make lyrics of prayer and poetry of thought. Thus can we hear music that in hymn and canticle, mass and oratorio, make us the heirs of Byzantium, the Renaissance and Elizabethan England; liturgies that enrich us with the spiritualities of a score of histories, from Mozarabic Spain to the Malabar coast of India. With all this we are gifted by the church's treasuring at least a measure of the vast riches of Jewish spirituality.

Yet having sought out such images by which to pay tribute to the church, I find myself turning to the vivid images of a particular moment in childhood to seal that tribute.

I was standing at the top of the courtyard onto which the front doors of about a dozen small houses opened. Ouside one of the doors the black crepe hung on the chipped paint. I was eleven. An elderly neighbor, Mrs. Griffin, was dying.

The Angelus was still ringing over the small city. I was standing holding a recovered ball. Suddenly around the corner shop at the end of the courtyard there appeared a huge, florid, black-cassocked priest. As if by prearranged signal, like an opera chorus appearing from the wings as a main actor moves center stage, doors opened and neighbors appeared. All play stopped. Addressing the street in general, the priest shouted, "Is she dead yet?"

The question ricocheted along the courtyard of houses, seeming to a child to achieve a quality greater than human inquiry. It was as if God was requiring a report on the condition of a soul. All the neighbors shook their heads. The vast figure turned and went up and over the hill beyond which the bell-booming tower stood against the evening sun.

For a child it was a many-layered moment. Only in adulthood would its complexity be unraveled. Even then, as with any mysterious encounter, unraveling will forever be partial.

Certainly there was the realization that somehow Mrs. Griffin was part of a communal world, her dying our shared terror and care, as her living had been part of a network of friendships and daily familiarities. There was a mingled message received about "the Church." On the one hand, it seemed to stand vast and unpitying, devoid of gentleness and any outward love. On the other hand, at some level of a child's being, there was communicated a great truth on that summer evening. It was, insofar as it can even now be expressed at all, a perception of a terrible matter-of-factness that seemed to indicate the presence of a power that refused to be impressed by the dread unseen visitor that inhabited the Griffin's house behind the draped door and the closed lace curtains and yellow blinds. In a child's mind there was placed a perception, as yet dimly understood, that while that ancient enemy would be allowed his time on our street, there was no longer cause for concern. Mrs. Griffin had already, so we all knew, been prepared by confession and shriving. She had been anointed with the oil of Extreme Unction. Death could be allowed the paltry booty of her aged body. Ancient and implacable boundaries of Word and Sacrament had been placed about his domains and arrogant claims.

The Angelus went silent. Front doors closed. The ball was thrown back into play. Mrs. Griffin's soul was secure among a community of children playing, as childhood does, on the boundary line of time and eternity. Later there would come the Requiem Mass, surrounding her with a community that possesses mysteries older and wiser and lovelier than the pitiable illusions we call time past, time present, time future.

We tend to think that faith comes on the constructed highway of teaching, study, information, thesis. Who knows by what unexpected byways of uncalculated and even un-remembered experience there comes a much deeper per-ception of what lies at the heart of things? I sometimes suspect that there are unnumbered bushes, ignited very early in our lives, that burn quietly and steadily for the warming of our hearts and the lighting of our way.

15. Passion for Pilgrimage

Nowhere is Celtic spirituality given a more natural setting than where I was standing. I was on a shingled beach beyond the town of Dingle, far out on the peninsula of the same name that forms part of the Kerry coastline facing the Atlantic.

The year was 1976. I had been there as a small child, later as a university student, then as a man in middle age. I was back in Ireland to celebrate the fiftieth wedding anniversary of my parents-in-law, and I was using a precious few days to drive through familiar places. Behind me to the east dark clouds were massing over the land. Out to sea the clouds ended, freeing the sun to spill yellow gold on the endless water. Caught between sunlight and shadow, the islands lay on the ocean, rounded headlands of dark green grass above brown rocks. Bordering everything were the writhing white waves. The largest island of the group was called Great Blasket.

Brendan, that fifth-century Celtic monk of whom tradition hints that he may have reached the shores of North America, stood on that coast looking at those islands, probably watching a gull as I did, hearing it scream harshly above the sound of the sea. Somewhere he must have heard in a gull's cry, as Moses heard in the blazing bush, the voice of God calling him to the journeys that fifteen centuries later would be mythic in a boy's school reader.

I see it now as a photograph indelible on the mind. There on the right-hand page of my schoolbook, a crude drawing occupied the top half of the page. A straight line signified the ocean's horizon. On the surface of the water was a long rounded curve. Three tiny figures were standing on the curved shape in the water, one bent down tending a small fire newly lit. A little distance away was a small single-sailed craft vaguely Norse in design. The few sentences on the schoolbook page, there to help us to learn reading, told us how a moment later the supposed island shuddered, threw the travelers into the water and disappeared. Thus we heard about Brendan and the island that was a whale.

Was I looking at that whale as I looked at the Great Blasket Island curving out of the ocean, rising high as my eye followed its contours returning to the sea again? Was it on that great still spine of rock that Brendan's monks lit their fire? Was the myth created because the island could disappear silently and swiftly in the driving rain in the Atlantic fog banks? Who knows or ever will know?

What we do know is that this and other islands along the Irish coasts have always called. For centuries they have been known as "the isles of the blest" or *Tir na n-Óg*, "the country of youth." Long before the new religion of the Cross came, they were the source of legend, islands of mingled erotic and fearful fantasy. In the pages of another schoolbook I would read the legend delineating the transition from the old gods to the new religion.

From the islands of the western sea came Neave of the Golden Hair, beautiful on her white horse. Encountering Finn and the heroic band of the Fianna, she invited Oisin the poet-warrior son of Finn to return with her, and he accepted. For what seemed to him a period of only three years Oisin was content to live in luxury in Tir na n-Óg. Then irresistibly Ireland called. He begged to return. He was given the white horse and told he could return but with one condition imposed on him: He must never dismount. How very early a child learned the lurking condition to all boons granted in mythic lands!

Oisin returned to Ireland to find that not three but three hundred years had passed. The Fianna were all gone, the great forests had diminished, people were smaller in stature, there was a new religion. Then, while bending to help a group of petty men lift a great stone, Oisin fell to earth. Instantly he aged to an old man near death and was brought to Saint Patrick for baptism before he died.

Thus did myth build bridges between the old and new gods. But there would be endless Oisins who would look west into the sun sinking into the ocean over the islands and see and hear a golden-haired siren calling them away. If it was a fatal legacy of the old gods, a revenge for their banishment by Patrick's god, they succeeded well, for there remained after them an undeniable urge to ocean pilgrimage that was to characterize Celtic Christianity for centuries.

The womb in which Patrick planted spiritual seed was a universe of rocky coasts and shimmering islands, all set in a cruel yet sometimes shining and lovely ocean. It lay on the edge of what men conceived to be the world, and so it lent itself particularly to the call of spiritual pilgrimage precisely because it offered the possibility not merely of going farther on the earth but of leaving it! To live on the margin of the world of men and women but to take ship from it is not merely to seek another world of men and women but to probe the worlds of demons, angels and, if one's craft is preserved from the ocean, to reach the crystal seas that in the dream journey of Saint John's Revelation surround the very throne of God himself.

One cannot dismiss this possibility lightly if one stands

on the Kerry coast looking out to Skelligs. The larger island, Skellig Michael, rears itself more than seven hundred feet out of the ocean. Between the mainland and the pillar of rock flow about seven miles of water hiding every mood from serenity to rage. Twice in my life I have tried this crossing and failed.

Sometime in the fifth century men crossed this seven-mile gulf. Given their cosmology, the setting out must have been similar to the kind of severance from earth as astronauts might feel today as the engines thunder to lift them into space. Somehow those fifth-century monks climbed the rock wall and built the stone beehive-shaped shelters that still stand today against the screaming wind.

If one is tempted to ask why in the name of God they did such a journey, the answer is probably already within the question. They journeyed precisely in the name of and in pursuit of nothing less than God. They had come to the conviction, held somewhere between the literal and the mystical, conscious and subconscious, that the western coast of this island, itself extending far out beyond a distant and darkening Europe, was the end of the world, and if so, it was then nothing less than a launching platform out of the world of time and space, a door into a different quality of geography, a new reality.

Somewhere in that innate sense of standing between two modes of reality were born many of the qualities that formed what is nowadays referred to as Celtic spirituality. That spirituality would not by any means remain merely Irish but would be the expression of a world that would inhabit not only this outer island but would survive the passing of the Roman legions from Britain and the coming of the Anglo-Saxons. It would retreat to the valleys of Wales, the moors and coasts of Devon and Cornwall, the

coasts of Brittany and of Northumbria, the Scottish islands. Its common geography would be the wilderness of
the sea, sometimes the high places of the old gods, the
hill or grove cleansed by Christian incantation, the old
sacrifices changed into the new mass.

Nor would Celtic spirituality remain in this bounded
world. Its passion for pilgrimage and its love affair with
the ocean would give it a restlessness. It would eventually
turn from the western ocean and head back for Europe
in missionary zeal. Its sails would catch breezes on the
Seine and the Rhine, its spades and ploughs dig the soil
of Alpine valleys, its chants sound beside the Danube, its
pens and brushes illuminate the walls of the first monas-
teries in Europe as well as in Ireland that would become
the embryos from which the Middle Ages would be given
birth.

But all this was still in the future when somewhere on
the western coast of Britain, early one morning in the
opening decade of the fifth century, a village awoke to the
shrieks and slaughter that meant a raid from the Irish
coast. Such raids had become common since the retreat
of the Romans.

Among the captives taken on the ship was a boy who
became a slave. Eventually he escaped but, haunted by the
island of his enslavement, he responded to its call. For
the rest of his life he moved about the island drawing the
tribes to the new religion. By the time of his death, the
island had given allegiance to the Crucified and Risen
One. Manannan, the god of the sea, had become the God
who had led a people through another sea. The Druidic
fires had died and were rekindled as Pentecostal flame. In
the green clearings in the forests there grew a tiny trefoil
that one day, named shamrock, would become the mythic

symbol of Patrick's achievement on behalf of his Triune God.

But as a light was kindled in the western sea, other lights in Europe faltered and died in a gathering darkness. Even as Patrick was dreaming of gaining freedom from his boyhood slavery, Alaric the Goth was riding into Rome and an age began to end. From Rome, agelong center of the west, the new religion looked now to the margins of the Western world where it would find two new centers. On the east shone the towers of the growing Byzantium capital of Constantinople, new Rome. To the west, in Ireland, were no shining towers, only a refuge made safe by its terrible isolation and a climate far more harsh than that of the Mediterranean.

On the east bank of the Shannon in the quiet midlands of Ireland, there are green fields where no sound louder than the lowing of cattle or the tractor engine is heard. There in the sixth century refugee Christians came from Europe, from Italy and Gaul and the Rhinelands. They sailed in tiny craft through the storms of Biscay, or down the Seine and the Rhine into the channel, out into the seas south of Britain and beyond into the treacherous tidal races between Cornwall and Ireland. Some even went round the outer island, risking the terror of the Atlantic, turning into the broad estuary of the Shannon and sailing upriver to Clonmacnoise.

There is little to be seen in Clonmacnoise now. But in the sixth century, drawn from all over Europe, there was a community of between three and six thousand, all of them making a costly commitment to the future. In the cluster of crude buildings that sheltered them, in the chatter of voices in excited debate, in the artists bent over their vellum manuscripts, in the reading of the Sacred

Word and in the acting out of the mystery of the Body and the Blood, in the planting and seeding and harvesting as they found by trial and error what would grow in this unfamiliar climate; in all these things they were bringing into being the elements that would seed the Middle Ages nearly half a millennium in the future.

Clonmacnoise was not alone but it was large. Other communities grew. There were rivalries, sometime even clashes. Tribalism died hard. In penance for one such encounter, a monk named Columba decided on self-exile. With a group of companions he acted out what was already a familiar pattern. The boat was built, the sail hoisted, the Te Deum sung and Columba and eleven companions, risking themselves to the ocean, ventured northeastward, finishing their voyage on the stony beach of Iona, a tiny island off the western coast of Scotland. From Iona they penetrated the fierce Pictish tribes on the Scottish mainland. From Iona for generations these Celtic christian monks moved fearlessly through the endless power struggles of northern England. Coming to yet another island beside yet another heartless sea, they settled down on Lindisfarne, the Holy Isle, in the North Sea off the Northumberland coast. There they built their rough walls and sang their hymns. The next two centuries saw them cross the North Sea to Europe, their sails returning from whence others had fled. Celtic missionaries would bring their arts, their husbandry, and their restless passion for faith into the heart of Europe, fertilizing its barren fields, penetrating its shadowed history with the sacred Light it had half forgotten, calling it Lazarus-like from the tomb of time.

To read what I have just written makes me realize that in the teaching of it to us as children, much more was communicated than mere information. There was also communciated a passion. Is that why I find that I have instinctively adopted a particular style and language? What could it be called—heroic? lyrical? As I look for a word, I realize that I write of these things now as an echo of what I heard as a child in their telling. I suspect that it is essentially the age-old style of the saga. To write of these things is to share a rune, to sing or to chant rather than to speak, to fashion cadence rather than to make mere statements.

The other realization that comes now in adulthood is that there was a sad implication in the way one was taught about these things. The implication, no less sad because true, was that those long-ago centuries were the paramount Irish contribution to history, a golden age when a small island and an isolated people were given their shining moment on the stage of history.

Such a perception may very well spring from the fact that, if one considers the centuries-long pattern of journeys that took travelers from Ireland, the reason for their going was far more often tragic than triumphant, far more often their having to flee from a situation than choosing to travel toward some eagerly anticipated task or purpose. Whether it was the flight of the Earls—the O'Neills and the O'Donnells—after the collapse of northern resistance to Elizabeth I or the flight of the wild geese—the defeated Jacobite allies under Patrick Sarsfield—or the terrible coffin ships that carried those trying to escape from the famine of the 1840s, so many anchors were weighed in tears and agony, in sadness and defeat, that it is perhaps only human that Irish history should treasure the memory of those sails of the sixth and seventh centuries, hoisted either in the pursuit of the unknown and mysterious or in fervent anticipation of spreading a sacred fire already kindled in the Celtic soul.

16. A Reason for Journeying

I was standing near the edge of the Cliffs of Moher in County Clare in western Ireland. It was August 1976. I was still on that hasty but intensely experienced car journey, grasping what remained of a vacation, realizing that there was so much of the past always waiting to be unraveled.

That rim of the world was a shimmering black wall falling seven hundred feet to the sea. Over it there blew a wind eternally alive, shifting at its undisciplined will to every corner of the compass, its voice rising and falling. Far below me the ocean heaved and bellowed, smashing itself against the base of the cliff, its frenzied frustration belying its implacable power to work its will over eons of time.

Sometimes the sky there was blue, the air clear, white clouds climbing from the southwest. More often it was as then, the damp mist swirling around the cliff face making it glisten like a towering marble wall ringing the world. The same mist forbade one looking far out over the ocean. Thus the boundaries of the world were drawn near, fashioned of mingled rain and spray and fog, closing like giant doors under whose dark threshold the ocean disappeared.

To stand there was to realize something of how climate and geography form an inner landscape in the human psyche as surely as they carve rocks and wear away mountains. To watch that ocean, to listen to that wind was to be called away mysteriously, sirenlike. Whether one stood there at Moher, the sweep of Galway Bay to the north, or far out at the end of the Dingle Peninsula on the Kerry coast looking out toward the Great Blasket Island; whether one walked a beach of Inishowen in Donegal watching the Atlantic sweep eastward for its wild surge south between the Giant's Causeway in Antrim and the coast of Scotland, always that siren voice called. Everywhere one was conscious that century after century those who stood there, including oneself, were called away, not swept by any apparent dark magic but going of their own volition, risking themselves to the future. It was as if all the reasons given for such going—missionary zeal, exploration, unemployment, restlessness, political exile, even famine—were all only disguises worn by a single seducer who sent a music on the wind, a Pan whose vast pipes sounded in the booming and whistle of the tides trapped in a thousand caves and inlets.

Century after century that call has sounded. It called Brendan and his company to coasts one day to be called Newfoundland and perhaps New England. It called the defeated O'Neills and O'Donnells to escape Elizabeth's revenge by fleeing south to sunny Valladolid. It called Jacobite fugitives in the late seventeenth century to the Catholic armies of Europe, some even to the emerging military struggles of South America. On and on went the procession over the waters; nineteenth-century Anglo-Irish families sending their sons to the armies of the Empire; others who looked like skeletons vomiting out their lives in seasickness and tuberculosis as they desperately sought to escape famine in the 1840's, praying for the slums of Boston to come over the horizon as a promised land for the hopeless. With them all went legions of Irish clergy, as surely identified with religion as Scots with engineering and English with administration.

I was a boy of twelve and Hitler had unleashed his

Panzers into Poland and Czechoslovakia. Agonizingly slowly England was gearing herself for the struggle, developing the industries that would eventually become her war machine. Those industries were seeking countless hands and eyes, skills and strengths to carry out the innumerable processes of a nation fighting for its life. In Cork, the small city where I lived, and all over Ireland, were tens of thousands of men and women in need of jobs, any jobs, in an economy pitifully inadequate to meet the demands and expectations of even the 1940s. For those men and women the cities of England became places of shining opportunity. The short sea voyage to the east became hope and agony, hope that money could be sent home by the one who went, agony because it meant exile in strange streets, among different accents, in a foreign land, a foreign faith.

The focus of all this hope and agony was the railway station, not far from where we lived. Each evening the crowds began to form to say goodbye to the family member who was going to England. From there they would take the train to Dublin, from there a ferry across the Irish Sea to Holyhead in Wales or to Liverpool. Some would take further trains to places like Manchester and Birmingham.

The crowds were huge, noisy, volatile, so much so that security dictated the closing of the heavy high gates at the station's entrance. Police were at the gates, on the edges of the crowd and inside the station. The wide road was almost totally blocked by the growing heaving mass of people. Through the middle, down a narrow passage carved out with difficulty, passed those actually traveling. Surrounded until the last possible moment by relatives, they were allowed through the gates and they disappeared in the cavernous shadows of the station. I remember my father pointing out to me as we watched one evening that a few people, immediate relatives, were allowed into the station area.

The layout of the station made possible something of immense poignancy. Within fifty yards or so of the platform's end there began a tunnel that then went for a mile or two under a hill and emerged beyond the city. The fact that the roadway where the crowd gathered went over the entrance to that tunnel made it possible for many to look down on the steaming engine and to see some sections of the long platform below them. Because of this, many of the crowd would hang over the low wall and try to communicate in hoarse crying shouts with some loved one. Below them the platform itself was a seething mass of humanity, totally possessed by grief.

The time would come when the last embraces would have to be broken, the guard would blow a long blast on his whistle, and the huge engine would let loose a vast cloud of steam. For a moment this steam would surround and hide the whole scene, as when in high melodrama the stage is hidden by smoke to hint of evil powers. As the great wheels spun with sudden spasms of power,the engine would loose a demonic shriek that rang in every eardrum. The crowd would shudder as a single entity, a deep low moan would sound in the gathering dusk, the long line of packed coaches would follow the engine into the night of the tunnel until the red light of the guard's van vanished into the swirling brown smoke.

Then would come a most pitiful moment. Sometimes a wife or mother, perhaps with a child, would lose control and run down the sloping end of the platform. Stumbling and shrieking her way toward the mouth of the tunnel, a demented Mary running to a tomb from which there seemed no hope of resurrection, she would be intercepted by police who as gently as possible would bring the distraught woman, often little more than a girl, back to her family or friends.

Thus the successive acts in a very ancient Irish drama would end. The station gates would again be opened by the tired and relieved police, those left behind on the platform would emerge, and others would gather around them. Soon the vast crowd would fade away over the hill into the city streets, many of the men to a public house for a drink, most of the women to little kitchens where small children waited and the Sacred Heart of Jesus, lit by its tiny scarlet-glassed flame, waited to receive a tearful prayer for the one gone.

My own calling away came very simply. It came in the form of a letter, nothing more, giving an invitation to work in Winnipeg, Manitoba. The invitation, at first refused, came again a year later, this time from Ottawa, Ontario.

The letter was ordinary but the origin of it was consistent with a generation's long pattern of Irish emigration, of links with the other side of the Atlantic. It came because there had been emigration of an earlier generation of the family after the First World War, so that now there were aunts and uncles, first and second cousins, somewhere in a distant Canada, visiting us periodically in black-and-white photographs where they stood in front of wooden verandas and Model-T Fords, both symbols (illusory as time showed) of an affluence beyond our wildest dreams.

The letter came because family correspondence had mentioned my ordination. In response to it, almost without realizing when or why the decision had been made, I found myself at the same railway station. Now I was not standing apart with my father watching a departing crowd. He had recently died. Indeed it is only as I write this that it occurs to me that his death may well have severed a tie, creating a call to journey.

The crowds were gone, their agony and the world's second war a decade-old memory. Yet I followed them, walking down the drab platform, saying a family goodbye, hearing the shriek of the whistle, feeling the shudder of the wheels' first turning, falling away into the yawning mouth of the tunnel, moving through the long minutes of pitch darkness punctuated by naked lightbulbs hanging on damp gleaming walls, emerging into a wide green glen familiar as a childhood playground, now spreading the sides of its valley in welcome and farewell like the arms of a midwife drawing forth a newly born child into an unfamiliar world.

For a while there were piercingly familiar places seen through the smoke-grimed window. The last suburban houses where friends lived, the small river where there were tiny minnows to be caught in a jam jar. We thundered by a farmhouse where I had played with a friend. After that the countryside began to flow away into the unfamiliar. Evening came, the compartment forming a tiny, swaying, dimly lit world where a book became refuge until fitful sleep assuaged the costly emotions of past weeks. Waking, I knew from the slow lurching of the train and the rows of tiny railway houses glimpsed in the wet glittering night that we were about to grind and squeal to halt under the echoing vault of the railway station in Dublin.

The decision to get a taxi was itself a break with the past. A taxi had always been synonymous with the unreality of Hollywood movies or, in real experience, with crises, illness, weddings, funerals. Down the dimly lit quaysides of the Liffey we moved, passing the looming magnificence of the Four Courts, near it Saint Michan's Church so familiar to Sean O'Casey. By crumbling Georgian doorways we moved, where George Bernard Shaw rummaged the secondhand bookstalls. Lights blazed and for a moment I looked down the wide avenue of O'Connell Street, so familiar from university. The dark streets closed again, old cobblestones hummed for a moment under the tires, and we were at the docks, the ferry looming above us.

The cabin was tiny, grey green, metallic. I looked out the porthole as a familiar world slipped into the rippling darkness. Thus I set out upon my own undistinguished and undramatic exodus, watching the water of my own Red Sea parted by the looming bow and the throbbing engines of this packet steamer, leaving behind the loved familiar people and places of my inner Egypt.

The next day in Liverpool the ferry across the Mersey was packed with early morning workers, grey faced and weary in the dawn. I glimpsed the Cunarder, red funneled, high in the water, majestic, its very name singing of distant and romantic places.

We did not sail until late afternoon. I was in a strange, unfamiliar city. I asked my way to the cathedral, having heard of its size and magnificence. In a never-to-be-forgotten experience I found that its massive and graceful form became grace to my vulnerability. I was at once diminished yet given identity as a child of God. My need was gently chided but at the same time nourished, my sadness and loneliness and fear were acknowledged and accepted even as they were placed among timeless and universal symbols of Cross, candlelight, altar, and Sacred Book. All had been part of the landscape of the inner

Egypt I was leaving yet all would, I knew, be in whatever wilderness of unfamiliarity lying ahead.

That wilderness appeared first as endless heaving waters, the white-topped, windblown, grey green mountains that range the north Atlantic with the approach of winter. Days passed before that restless wilderness assumed a mask of serenity and I was gazing across the Strait of Belle Isle at the gleaming coast to the north. Mile after distant mile it fell away slowly. Evening came and sleep, and in the morning along the nearer coast of Quebec there appeared the first villages, pitched between the river and the land, the latter stripped of its fall colors and readying itself to receive the white armor of winter. In every village the spire of the parish church, pointing upward and painted in gleaming silver, measured my wondering journey as the waters of the Saint Lawrence bore me to a new birthing.

The endless land rising away to the north recalled the voice of a priest whom I had first heard as a small boy in Saint Mary's in Castlecomer and later as a youth in boarding school. As a deputation secretary for one of the many missionary societies, Canon Adcock traveled around Ireland, visiting parishes and communicating boundless energy and ageless enthusiasm, both of which were, of course, very attractive qualities to the young.

Year by year the canon would return to Midleton, the small town in County Cork where our boarding school was. On the appointed evening we would be lined up two by two, everyone armed with a penny for the inevitable collection. Down the village street we would march under the watchful yet benevolent eye of the duty master. Filing into the bare boards and timeworn chairs of the two-roomed school in the town, we would be given a "magic lantern" lecture, the lantern in question of course being the ancestor of today's slide projector. Housed in black metal, the eye of its huge heavy lens protruding, the simple machine received large glass slides that then appeared on the white sheet hung against the end wall as images of western Canada.

We were gazing at them in the early 1940s. I realize now that we were then looking at the western Canada of the 1920s and 1930s. As each slide appeared, the voice of the canon would tell us stories of his years there, his voice increasing in passionate recollection as the fleeting hour went by. Since he stood behind us to work his magic lantern, I now recall his voice as if in some sense disembodied, godlike, speaking of snow and woods and prairie, a wilderness in which lay isolated towns and tiny communities where apparently the work of God awaited those willing to go.

When all was over, each received a small collection box. Shaped as a tiny log cabin complete with chimney stack, its roof was covered by a gummed label proclaiming it to be the possession of the Commonwealth and Continental Church Missionary Society. It was the label, simply and even crudely drawn, that haunted me. Across the center of the paper was a straight line that signified a distant horizon. At the left side stood a solitary coniferous tree. From the left there came a heavily clothed figure driving a dog team pulling a sled. In the yellow-paper sky above the horizon line, there hung a single-engined plane. Etched indelibly in a boy's imagination, the scene drew more than the weekly penny in faithful offering. It drew oneself. Years later it would appear again as I stood on the deck of a liner moving down the calm waters of a soon-to-be-frozen Saint Lawrence. In later life I would see a thousand times the device of television producers that draws a viewer into the picture using a zoom lens. Whenever I see that device, it is into that long-ago simple picture I am drawn, hearing the barking of dogs, the hiss of runners on snow, the drone of a distant engine.

There is another photograph engraved in my mind, that of an uncle, always since a favorite uncle, that essential ingredient of childhood. The photograph was first discovered in childhood on the farm. My uncle had for a few years gone to America, working on the farm of a relative. One day while he was working in the fields the photograph was taken. He was standing by a tractor, clad in open shirt, britches and leggings, his black hair tousled, a wide-brimmed hat held casually by his side. One foot and one hand were on the tractor. He was in his twenties, handsome and smiling. I would often look at it, gazing at it, entering in through the doorway of the thin white border surrounding that distant world and time. By some magic known only to a child, I would not only go to him but I would become him. I would feel my legs held by those leather leggings, my eyes narrowed and steady against the sun. With a flourish I would don my sweat-soaked hat, swing myself up into the seat, grasp the great black steering wheel, turn the key to bring the engine to a snarling roar. Swaying and lurching over the rich rough earth, I would drive out across the endless fields watching the golden grain blowing and tumbling under my thundering knives.

As I write these things in an Alberta rectory study, I am set in the reality of contemporary western Canada. I walk betwen gleaming urban highrises that reflect the sun as it sets behind the blue white-topped wall of the Rockies. A few minutes driving brings me to rolling country, a world golden with grain or white with snow according to its season.

By such a journey, called by such images and voices, I came to another land, unknown yet strangely familiar from childhood dreaming. On the Feast of All Saints 1954 I entered the chapel of Christ Church Cathedral, Ottawa, Ontario, with the then Dean, John Anderson, whose letter had brought me there. We knelt to say the Office of Matins. For a moment there was silence. A quiver of loneliness and fear invaded the stillness. Suddenly I heard him say, "O Lord, open thou our lips." In response I said, "And our mouth shall show forth thy praise."

Two and a half thousand years ago a poet had first sung those lines as one of the Psalms of David. For sixteen hundred years they had welcomed the dawn in unnumbered monastery chapels. For over four hundred years they had been Thomas Cranmer's gift to the Book of Common Prayer. For twenty-six years they had punctuated the changing rhythms of my growing. Now on this morning of new beginning they spoke of eternal realities that bound together the torn geography of my life, making it again whole.

JUL 23 '85

BX 5620 .O37 A33
O'Driscoll, Herbert.
A doorway in time

J06249

SS $11.95

WITHDRAWN

13-11/88   14-)12/98

Please Do Not Remove Card From Pocket

YOUR LIBRARY CARD

may be used at all library agencies. You
are, of course, responsible for all materials
checked out on it. As a courtesy to others
please return materials promptly. A service
charge is assessed for overdue materials.

The SAINT PAUL PUBLIC LIBRARY